Short Stories of Hope

Compiled and Edited by Caroline Boxall

Published 2024

Box of Books Publishing

Short Stories of Hope

Written by Children for Children

*Where there's **hope**, there's life. It fills us with fresh courage and makes us strong again.*

Anne Frank

To enter the 2025 competition please visit
https://www.carolineboxall.com/competition

Compiled and edited by Caroline Boxall 2024

The Authors

Many congratulations to the talented winners of the
2024 Short Story Competition.

The authors attend the following schools:
Al Yasmin International School, Riyadh, Kingdom of Saudi Arabia
The Royal Masonic School
St Pauls C of E Primary, Kings Langley
Northwood College
Parmiter's Watford
St Peters Catholic Primary, Leatherhead
Cherry Tree Primary, Watford
Wood End School Harpenden
Chorleywood Primary
Beechfield School, Watford
The Beacon School, Amersham

Making dreams come true...

As a child, I dreamed about becoming a writer and, one day, seeing my books published - out there for the world to read.

My dream came true in 2020 when my first book was published. It was just as exciting as I had imagined. Seeing my words in print and knowing that complete strangers were reading them was thrilling.

In 2023, I launched the first Creative Writing Competition, open to children aged 8-13. The prize was publication in this book. The stories could be up to 500 words in length, all with the theme of Hope.

I was thrilled to receive well over 100 entries from all over the world – as far as Saudi Arabia! I loved reading all of them, but a competition's a competition, and the talented writers included in this book are the worthy winners.

Thank you to everyone who entered. I've already launched the 2025 competition, so I'm hoping for even more entries from even further afield.

Do you know a child who would like to enter?

More details at https://www.carolineboxall.com/competition

SUBSCRIBE

Books by Caroline...

The Runaway Children of Chennai

The Secret Children of Mumbai

The Secret Life of Dmitri Molchalin

The Mole of Moscow, June 2024

The Fox of Sevastopol, November 2024

The Snake of Southwold, 2025

The Chameleon of Carisbrooke 2025

The Raven of Paris, 2026

Crazy Creatives – how to write a brilliant short story, October 2024

Subscribe to Caroline's blog so you don't miss the next book

www.carolineboxall.com

Contents

Hello

By Matilda Gardner - age 11

Picking up my phone I excitedly tapped out a message to Kyra, my bestie.

Can't wait to see you tomorrow. No reply.

Maybe a sleepover this weekend? No reply.

I had barely seen my best friend over the holidays. Apart from walking our dogs once, she always seemed busy. I was looking forward to the first day of school - we'd chat about the summer and share all our news.

In the morning I got dressed proudly in the school uniform, complete with my BFF necklace, which Kyra had bought for me on my birthday.

On my way to school, see you soon. No reply.

When I arrived, I searched for Kyra in our normal meeting spot, but she wasn't there. I waited by myself for a few minutes and then I saw her. She was in a big group surrounded by the so-called "cool girls". Why was she there? All they did was gossip about new make-up and skincare. I went over to her, nerves rushing through me, and pretended not to notice the other girls backing away and sniggering.

"Hi!" I said brightly. "Was your summer good?"

"Yeah, I guess," she replied quietly, staring blankly at the floor. I was about to carry on the conversation, but the other girls swarmed around her like wasps and they strutted away, leaving me alone.

A week passed. I hadn't spoken to Kyra and when I tried, she just stared somewhere else and replied dismissively. Every day I felt petrified about coming to school and being alone again. Kyra has been surrounded by the "cool girls" and I was starting to lose hope that we would ever talk again. I wished that everything could have just gone the way I hoped for. I'd probably be round Kyra's house, endlessly bouncing on the trampoline, but instead I was up in my room alone.

The next day, I was walking to my Maths lesson when I heard someone calling my name. Immediately, I turned around, hoping it was Kyra. But no, it was Amaya, the new girl. She seemed quite nice, but she keeps asking me things when I didn't want her or anyone else talking to me.

She saw me, walked faster towards me and asked how my day had been.

"Um good I think," I replied faintly, not really wanting to talk.

At home I burst into tears and told my mum everything. How Kyra wouldn't hang out with me anymore, and how Amaya had been bugging me.

"Evelyn," Mum said in her gentle way. "Maybe Amaya is also alone and feels the same as you."

The next day, during break I saw Amaya standing alone. She looked sad and I realised that my mum was right. I caught a glimpse of Kyra laughing with her new gang, and then looked back at Amaya. I walked towards her and watched her face light up as she noticed me.

"Hello."

The Drummer

By Hazel Denham - age 11

I gazed out of my window at the sunset which beamed its rays back at me. Slowly, the light began to fade, disappearing behind the horizon. Quiet as a mouse, I cracked my door open, tiptoed down the stairs and, feeling a pang of guilt, eased out of the front door. I just wish my parents could understand. But too worried about grades and exams, they never would. Shaking it off, I leapt aboard my rickety bike and cycled to the town bins.

Wrinkling my nose against the stench of rotten food, I transformed the lids and containers to create what I needed. Well practised now, I could assemble my makeshift drum kit at lightning speed. Taking a deep breath, I started. Lost in my drumming, I was hit in the face by a ball of paper. "Ugh!" I cried, snatching it from the floor. I was about to tear it up when I read the title: Music Competition!! This was my chance and, if I could win this, maybe my parents would understand what music was to me!

Back in my bedroom, I hung the poster on the wall, wishing I could tell my parents about the contest, but they'd never let me go. I started humming my rhythm as I slotted in elements like a jigsaw puzzle. My eyes were just starting to close as the song finally locked into my head.

On the night, I cycled to the local stadium. Standing in the wings, I felt the other musicians' music - it tugged at my heart strings whilst at the same time my optimism crashed down around me. I felt sick to my stomach - I was no musician - just a girl who banged on bins.

"I - I can't go on," I told the stage manager. But all he gave me was a thumbs-up and a small push to get me on stage. With butterflies in my stomach, I picked up the drumsticks and began. Suddenly, two familiar figures made their way to the front of the crowd clutching my poster in shaky hands: my parents - they were here! Unsure, I lost my rhythm. I stopped playing.

The crowd started to whisper. I felt like crying. I wanted to go home. Why did I think I could do this? But then, one by one people started to clap my rhythm and soon the stadium was alive with my song. I looked at my parents; they were stamping and clapping to my beat along with everyone else! I sat down again and started to drum, losing myself to the music.

Before I knew it, I was done. A huge cheer echoed across the whole stadium and soared into my heart. I ran from the stage and into my parents' arms. As we embraced, I started to cry: my music had brought people together. Suddenly winning the competition didn't seem so important. I could see the pride in my parents' eyes and that was enough.

Your Heart With Mine

By Annabel Radburn - age 13

Walking home with Abby made everything disappear; when it was just us, I mean, not all her popular friends. Abby was perfect; beautiful, talented and kind. She was going to win Prom Queen for sure. I was happy for her, my best friend after all. Sometimes, I just couldn't help the envy. But it would be enough to stand next to her and her prom crown, I supposed.

We reached my house, just up the road from hers. 'Bye Bec, your heart with mine!' Abby's little catchphrase, as if to make me feel important. I never understood it. But her sweet voice made it special.

'Hey Rebecca!' Mum shouted, slightly manic, as I walked in.

'Hey', I replied flatly. Something was wrong. Her voice only did that masked enthusiasm when involving Inez. Inez, my sister, younger by one year. Cardiomyopathy ruined her. Ruined me as well. She was diagnosed at the age of fourteen and is on the list for a heart transplant. I love her, but it's taken everything. If I left, would my parents even notice? The one fun thing I'd arranged with Mum was prom dress shopping, cancelled because Inez found a possible donor. Didn't work out though. 'What's wrong mum?' I asked, trying to be understanding. 'She's worse again today.' I knew how bad it was, of course. If Inez didn't find a donor soon, she wouldn't make it.

My safety blanket was Abby. When we talked, the problems faded. But when we chatted about prom walking to school the next morning, a shameful part of me hoped that flawless Abby wouldn't go. Walking along, she was looking at dresses online. She'd found a stunning red satin one. That's when I got what I had hoped for so selfishly. Red Fiat car, the same colour as her prom dress. The same colour as her blood. She stepped out. I remember a scream, squealing car brakes, and the sound of the ambulance. My safety blanket, so unsafe, so dead.

Not immediately. Somehow she hung on for three excruciating days, strung up like a puppet in intensive care. Heart still beating, yet no longer with mine.

But the puppeteer's hopes were nothing but dreams. Under my disgusting blanket, I watched Grey's Anatomy like it would bring Abby back every time Meredith saved someone. Suddenly Mum was there, insensitively ecstatic. 'Inez found a donor!'

No one told me, but I wasn't surprised by that. 'I know you're upset Rebecca' Mum said gently. 'Maybe you'd like to take Inez to the prom? I'll take you both dress shopping. 'Okay,' I said, each syllable hurting my throat.

I picked a pale yellow dress with flowers around the hem. Inez chose a red satin one.

'Are you ready?' she asked, as I steadied her into the car. 'Come on,' Inez coaxed and hugged me tight. 'As long as we're together we'll be fine.' She grabbed my hand, beautiful in her blood-red satin dress.

'Let's do this Bec. Your heart with mine.'

A Hike to the Peak

By Aaisha Asfiya - age 10

I looked up at the hill!

"It's so huge. Will I reach the peak...?" I was terrified, yet began to climb despite all my fears.

Sweat was rolling down my cheek, and exertion and tiredness began to overcome me with each uphill step.

Then I stopped to rest.

I did not realize that my team was far ahead, "How could they just go without noticing me?"

I drank some water, munched a handful of snacks, and continued climbing, but this time faster and more determined. I decided not to stop. One should see the determination on my face. It all lasted for a couple of hours. Then, I looked down and felt proud of myself.

"Oh... Only a few more steps left!" I whispered.

After some time, I found myself standing atop a huge mountain.

With closed eyes, I declared, "How well I improved from a girl who was afraid of heights to the one who climbed all the way to the peak!"

A year ago, on a Friday evening, my friend's family and I had been to an amusement park. There, I'd had to face the most dreadful experience of my life.

Yes, it was a rollercoaster!

My friend complained, "You are exaggerating a rollercoaster to a giant monster!" But for me, it was a life-threatening game!

Everyone wanted to ride the coaster, while I stumbled with fear. I was so scared and wanted to return home immediately instead of riding that horrible thing! However, I did not want to be called a scary cat and thus tried my best to keep calm.

My only thought during that ride was: "What if the ride stops in mid-air?"

I started to scream like a maniac until my voice was completely gone. From that day, my fear told me to stay away from heights.

"But today, I denounced all my fears of yesteryears!" I felt proud of myself for reaching the peak despite missing my team.

I was overwhelmed by the cool breeze. My body felt as light as air. I sat down to continue enjoying the moment. The breeze twirled around me, making me feel like I was flying. It made me fall asleep.

Not so long after, I was woken up by the loud noises and laughter of children. Everyone on my team was standing around me.

"Are you okay?" the leader asked.

I jumped up and down, confirmed I was alright, and asked them to calm down and start the descent. We had a laughing blast until they dropped me at my home.

I entered the house and found my brother raging angrily for not taking him along.

The Disappearance

By Amelia Kumuthan - age 13

When I was six, my mum left me. I don't know why she left or where she went, she just left. It was a confusing time for me, trying to comprehend why someone who was supposed to love me unconditionally would vanish without a trace. In the years that followed, I grew up with my dad who did his best to fill the void my mum's absence had left behind. But no matter how hard he tried, there was always a lingering sense of emptiness in our home. As I grew older, my feeling of hope in finding my mother corrupted me. I became obsessed with uncovering the truth about my mum's disappearance. I spent countless hours poring over old photographs, searching for any clue that might lead me to her. But each lead turned out to be a dead end, and the mystery only deepened with time. But I never lost hope.

It was that fateful day, on my eighteenth birthday, something very unexpected happened. A letter arrived in the mail addressed to me. It was written in my mum's handwriting, a handwriting I had studied countless times in those old photographs. My hands shook as I tore open the envelope, my heart pounding with anticipation.

Inside was a single piece of paper, with just a few words scrawled across it: "Meet me at the old oak tree by the river, tonight at midnight, I'll explain."

My mind raced with questions. Was this really from my mum? And if so, why had she waited all these years to reach out to me? Despite my doubts, I couldn't ignore the chance that this might finally provide the answers I had been searching for.

That night, I slipped out of the house while my dad slept soundly, making my way through the darkness to the old oak tree by the river. As I approached, a figure emerged from the shadows, and my breath caught in my throat. It was her, my mum, looking just as she had in those old photographs, but there was something wrong. Tears welled up in my eyes as I rushed forward to embrace her, but before I could reach her, she held up a hand to stop me.

"I'm sorry I have to do this Amelia." Her voice was soft and scared, like a little mouse facing its predator. As she spoke, my confusion only grew. What did she mean by having to do this? Before I could utter a word, she continued, her eyes darting nervously around the dimly lit clearing.

"I know you must have a million questions, but there's something you need to understand," she began, her voice trembling. "I didn't leave because I didn't love you. I left to protect you."

Her words hung in the air, heavy with meaning. Protect me? From what? I wanted to demand answers, but something in her expression made me hold my tongue. She reached into her pocket and pulled out a small, worn-out locket. With shaking hands, she opened it, revealing a faded photograph inside. It was a picture of a man I had never seen before, yet there was something hauntingly familiar about him.

"This is your father," she whispered, her voice barely above a whisper. "And he's not who you think he is."

Hope

By Aisha Lawton - age 13

Have you ever wondered how your brain works and the different emotions and feelings in it? Well part of that is me, stuck inside your brain. The wavy lines everywhere, the roots down the roads of the brain. But in one office, in the left east corner, there works the emotions and me. I make you light up with joy. I am the feeling that warms you inside.

I am Hope.

I might not have been born in your brain yet, or I might have died in your brain, but there is always a way to bring me back. I am created by the small figure of Inspiration, my fellow friend who lives near me. I make goals into a vision of the future.

I think I have quite a cool, but tricky job in the brain.

My friend Inspiration and I work like peanut butter and jam. You see, I am the one who creates the fire, but he is the one to create the spark. You might be wondering what keeps the fire alive: Happiness.

Happiness is the main key to the fire. She keeps the spark alive and makes sure that Hope and Inspiration stay in the fire, because without one of us, none of us work. As one of the main roles in this fire, I have to make sure I do my job properly and you are probably wondering how this works.

I am a bit like a police officer who keeps all the negativity and sadness out, but keeps the inspiration and happiness alive. It's like a battle, or you might know it as a voice in your head saying you can't have hope, inspiration or happiness.

I believe, with me and the gang fighting these bad thoughts, we can create positivity in your brain and in your life.

Day in and day out, I work my hardest to keep everyone's brains firing and ready to go down the right track.

So, next time a bad thought appears in your head, think of me and my friends and all of the work we do in your mind to make you have hope.

Don't let the hard work go to waste.

In Between Light and Dark there is Hope

By Shrinika Kashyap - age 11

Another gloomy day in Autumnvale and Alice had just woken up. She sighed as she got dressed and went downstairs for breakfast.

"Good morning, Alice. Your dad and I are going to work. Be good!" Alice's mum said, not focusing on Alice.

For her, it was the same activities every day. Wake up, eat, sleep. Autumnvale was most likely the gloomiest town on Earth.

Alice went over to Maya's house, her best friend, who lived next door. They had known each other since kindergarten. Alice felt nice talking to Maya, because she understood how she felt. They both wanted to change how blunt the days were. They never stopped hoping that one day, they would wake up to a colourful, bright place where they could be as happy as can be.

Alice and Maya were talking as usual, when they heard faint music from a distance. They had heard it many times before, but this time

Alice said, "I've had enough of sitting around. Let's check the noise out."

Maya replied with, "Sounds fun."

They followed the joyful music until it was so close that they could hear people singing along to it. Alice couldn't read Maya's mind, but she could tell from her face that she would move to this new town in a heartbeat. They walked to the end of the town and went over the fence quickly. Their mouths dropped open.

The place was full of arcades and balloons were flying around. Actors in costumes were talking to little kids whilst they ate fluffy cotton candy. A rollercoaster spiraled and coiled like an elongated snake twisting through the event. Exhilarated screams and cheerful shouts of friends greeting one another.

Maya and Alice ran around like mad monkeys, using the £5.00 pocket money they always kept. Alice wasted their money on two cotton candies for both of them, whilst Maya used money for an arcade and two roller coaster tickets. They had never had this much fun before.

Many hours later of just wandering around, Maya commented that they should be getting back by now. And they did, sadly.

"We *need* to tell everyone about this. They might change their mind. Our dream might finally come true," said Alice. Maya agreed, so they skipped back. As soon as Alice and Maya got back, they heard voices.

"Hey, look! Two little girls crossed over to another town, away from here," yelled a gruff man. Other people moved closer to hear more. Nobody would ever cross towns here. But here was the girls' chance to speak to the many people in the crowd. With hope in their hearts, they began explaining how they felt.

"It's good to have fun sometimes," said Maya.

Some agreed and some didn't. They came with Alice and Maya the next day. Some people weren't happy with the idea. Others had gone and seen it and they loved it. Their dream that had once been a thought, came true.

Sort of.

The Cittrusy Cipher

By Vanisha Barot - age 11

There was once a girl who always dreamed of being a detective, but Naomi never thought it'd come true. One night, she opened her bag to uncover a letter with a hint of lemons. It was empty, but she felt something. She brought a matchbox, and so her case began.

Slightly burning the page, the words started to reveal themselves as she continued.*Help me, I am in trouble. Do what I ask, or I will die.*

Shocked, she read on.*Go to a place where you are not allowed to make too much noise and you can study. In between the truth of King George and King Henry, there will be a piece of paper: the blueprint! You have to find it quickly!*

Naomi considered her options. Only one place fitted the description: the library! As soon as dawn rose, she raced to the library. The truth of two kings, she wondered, were possibly in the history section? Eventually, she found the two adjacent books and the blueprint which was wedged so tightly you could barely see it.

Along with the plan, she found another empty page. Back at her house, she burned the letter and could not believe what she saw. *Let me introduce myself, I am Anaya, your long lost sister. I have given you this responsibility, as I have been watching you for a long time. You'll need to go somewhere. A place where a certain type of drink is made.*

But what was the place she was talking about?

As she went to search for an idea on Doodle, she found a video with a face which looked very similar to hers. It could be her sister. She was repeating the words, "Save me, save me," but towards the end of the video, her face faded and she caught a glimpse of a bottle of lemonade. Lemonade, she thought. Where can you find lemonade? She replayed the video and found, around the bottle, a small logo on the wrapper which she recognised. Then, it clicked. By her house, just a few miles away, was a factory which made the sweetest lemonade.

She ran there straightaway, and burst through the doors, only to find people who looked nothing like the face she had seen on the screen. They were all me wearing plain black uniforms with a logo on the top right corner of their chest. After staring silently at all of their faces, something caught her eye. One person was wearing a bright blue t-shirt, who was, in fact, a girl! But she couldn't see the girl's face properly. What if it was the wrong person? Was she imagining things or was this real? She walked up to the girl to get a closer look. She saw her face, and she couldn't believe her eyes. It was really her! She was bubbling with emotions.

Naomi quietly took Anaya out of the crowded factory. "Thank you so much," said Anaya

Naomi smiled. "How did you get in there?"

Anaya replied, "I was kidnapped by somebody who saw me using my magic tricks many years ago. You were really small back then. Did our parents not tell you?"

"No, they didn't, " replied Naomi, visibly confused.

"What's wrong?"

Naomi responded, "Why did nobody tell me about you?"

"I don't know, Naomi. But now let's just get to know each other properly and do everything that sisters do."

"Deal."

The Slumber

By Alba Riley - age 11

I was tucked up in bed, my eyes were closing. I could feel my head sinking into my pillow as I began to fall asleep. I loved this part of the day, somewhere between fantasy and reality - dreaming with no strings attached.

As I lay peacefully without a care in the world, suddenly the whole room shifted and I found myself somewhere else. What was a peaceful place in my head had transformed into somewhere empty. My senses were on high alert as I noticed a figure walking towards me. Feeling nervous, I spoke out a quiet, 'Hello'.

As she moved closer, I saw a girl, she looked the same age as me. Anxious to know who she was, I repeated 'Erm, hello, I'm lost, can you help me?' Staring straight into my eyes I saw that she was confused.

'Hi' she said 'My name is Hope, I think the exit is that way,' she pointed, 'let's walk there.' She explained that she had been walking for a long time and I was the first person she had seen in a few hours.

As we walked together, Hope said the last thing she remembered was falling asleep and waking up here - where was 'here' I wondered?

Then I remembered, I too had fallen asleep and I realised that this wasn't reality - we were trapped in a dream!

Together, we decided we needed to think. As we closed our eyes to concentrate, we heard a sudden bang. Jumping up, we saw a window open - we couldn't reach it so we decided to make a plan. Hope was taller than me and we agreed I would stand on her shoulders and pull myself up. Just reaching, I was able to climb through and stretch back for Hope and pull her up. Our team work gave me hope that we would find a way out together.

Looking around, all we could see was mirrors. There were millions of us both, but I could still see who was the real version. Running to her, I said we should keep on moving - she gave me a simple nod. As we walked through the mirrors, to entertain ourselves we swapped necklaces. Hope had an H and I had an G for Grace..

In the distance, we could see one mirror had a sign that said 'Exit'. 'We've made it,' I shouted. We ran towards the exit and as I reached out and touched the mirror my hand disappeared though it! I looked at Hope and said 'I guess this is goodbye.' We smiled, and I passed through the mirror.

The next thing I remember, is waking up with Mum in my room saying, 'Come downstairs we have someone to meet, our new neighbours', Disorientated, I followed downstairs passing a mirror and seeing the H necklace! Startled, I walked into the room and saw a family, as they turned around, I recognised the young girl....

Was it a dream?

The Magic Library

By Emilie Menhinick - age 9

This isn't an ordinary story. No.

You could see the elaborate designs all over the walls and ceiling. Huge chandeliers were hanging down and you could smell all the pages of the books waiting to be read. Stella and Peter made their way up to the third level and tugged out a book. It looked like an ancient book that had been there for centuries. The librarian, Mr Draziw came up to them with an interesting look. "Ah, you have found the book of magic," he smirked.

They both exchanged looks then Stella said, "Magic isn't real."

"Suit yourself."

Then, just as they opened the book, they were sucked into a ginormous portal.

Suddenly, beams of light came shooting out from every direction and they both hit the ground with a thud.

"Where are we?" asked Peter with a puzzled look on his face.

"I think we just got sucked into a ginormous portal," said Stella with an even more confused look.

"Do you think Mr Draziw knew about this portal?" asked Peter .

“Of course," replied Stella. "That's why he was looking funny. He's probably going to follow us through the portal. Here he comes, hide!”

Lying on the ground was Mr Draziw, looking like he was in pain. “Finally, after twenty years, I am back in Fantasia. All I need to do now is to follow those kids to find the magic key.”

Then he turned around and started his journey.

“What key?” whispered Peter.

"Probably the one that makes you the most powerful person in the world. Says right here in this book!” exclaimed Stella. "We have to get to it before Mr Draziw.".

So, off they went on their adventure. Soon enough they came across a meadow filled with mushrooms, but they came to an abrupt stop, because Mr Draziw was on the other side.

“Why does Mr Draziw want to be very powerful?”

And just then, Stella solved it. Draziw spelled backwards is Wizard...

Spark of the Flowers

By Caitlin Johnston –Weston - age 13

Some think hope is stupid, and that there is no point in something that will let you down time and time again. Those people haven't had hope yet, not really. When you feel that spark ignite in your chest, that dream that might be possible, that is when you have hope.

So, what happens to the girl who could dream? The girl who could hope? What happens if she loses that passion that kept her going? So, what happens when the light that was always on flickers out?

Dahlia was a normal girl, in a once normal city. Though the world was anything but. She couldn't remember her last name anymore. Who would, when encompassed by darkness, day, and night? Her dreams didn't exist, they were crushed, along with the building that was home to some of the best teachers in the world. She would not go to this university, because it was gone. So was light, and everything that Dahlia had loved. Her apartment was too small and too big all at the same time. It was blackout time, just as it always was. The New Alliance, as they called themselves, were ruthless, not having so much as a shred of mercy. Dahlia despised the name; everyone thought it was stupid. It was. They knew nothing of alliances.

It was 2054 and Dahlia was alone, her parents killed by the bombs that were dropped all over the world. She was 19, and she was supposed to be at the University for the Gifted, studying her only passion - journalism. The rations that were supplied were running out and no one could offer a solution. Someone would have to sort out this situation eventually, but even the smartest people couldn't. Almost no one covered windows anymore, there was no need when the darkness had swept across the globe. So Dahlia sat alone on her sofa that she couldn't even see and ate the food that was running out.

It was a normal day. Or as normal as it could be. *Blink. Blink. Blink.* She didn't know what was happening. Forcing herself to open her eyes wide, she saw something so terrible, so dangerous that she could be dead within the minute, and yet Dahlia did not feel scared, she did not feel timid. She felt a light that was thought to be long gone come back, because it did. There was a light on. A light, something so full of hope, but also with despair.

Dahlia almost fell off her sofa. It was a magnificent shade of blue. She stumbled to her mahogany door like a baby learning to walk for the first time. Dahlia opened the door to her apartment and trudged down the corridor to the next one. She knocked.

It opened

"Hello, I'm Violet, Violet Schulz."

"Your light is on."

"Yes, it is."

And from there a fire would ignite across the globe.

The Uprising

By Nivethan Ambikaiseelan - age 11

It is the year 2033. Nothing but the Tower of Vile stands in the stark, alienated, desolate, once thriving nation. Along each dark alleyway, groups of mice scurry, as dust and cobwebs begin to build up. Every street is a reminder of the defeat from five years ago, one that led to the captivity of humankind. No one can smile, no one can dream of happiness, no one can yearn for freedom. Everybody is enslaved by Lord Vile. They are waiting for a beacon of hope.

"I hate doing these tiring chores every day, but nobody can rebel against Lord Vile. If only there was a way. If only I could gain the courage to fight for my people. If only I could..."

A deafening cough echoed through the chamber, interrupting my thoughts. "Dad, are you alright?" I asked.

“Yes son. Everything is alright...” my Dad began, "...but my time is coming to an end, because of this sickening disease. I’m giving the responsibility of taking care of the family to you.”

“Dad, don't talk that way. We will all leave this tower together, as a family. Don't talk negatively. We will work something out, we always do!” I responded, trying to fight the truth.

"Son, you are now of the age where I no longer have to hide my feelings, just to improve your happiness. You must accept that my time is up. However, I will not allow myself to perish, before becoming a beacon of hope. Take this device, son. When the time comes, I will make a distraction for you. I will not tell you when, but you will know. Click this button and we will be free," he whispered.

"Silence!" a shadow commanded.

The figure's presence alone shook the souls of all around. His flowing dark cape complementing the evil in his soul. It was Lord Vile. But Dad was not shaken; he was ready to fight back.

As Lord Vile turned around, Dad sprung. With overwhelming speed and agility, he pulled a knife from his pocket, and with all his power, he struck.

But it was useless. Vile turned with a malicious smile, caught Dad's hand midair and sniggered, "How pathetic! I can almost cry out of laughter. And now you will set an example for the rest of your kind" Lord Vile proclaimed.

He twisted my dad's hand, but Dad kicked Vile in the face, cracking the armour beneath and, without him noticing, stuck a destructive device to his neck.

A tsunami of emotions flooded me as I realised what was about to happen. My legs wouldn't move. All the joyful memories of my family flashed before me as Dad whispered, "Now!"

Dad struck the ground, motionless, as Lord Vile cheered with maniacal laughter, but I knew what had to be done: I targeted the nape of his neck and clicked.

Bang! Fumes of smoke appeared. When it cleared, Vile was gone. My father had shone the first rays of hope, and now I amplified it. Happiness and screams of joy echoed. Everyone paraded with glee. We were finally free.

The Choices We Make

By Siena Pitney - age 12

Hi, I'm Faith. Just a sick girl at an orphanage, in search of a cure. My sister Hope and I overheard strangers talking about 'a miracle worker' who could remove all traces of my ailment. Luckily, they dropped a business card so we hurried to pick it up. It read: Bring £100. Find me. E16AF, London.

We desperately needed that £100. With no choice, we fled the orphanage and set off, determined to find him. We scavenged for cash, but only found £63.25. Feeling defeated, we entered the station, greeted with the stench of sweat, smoke and urine.

Despite our fatigue, we bolted to the platform, stepping in partly-chewed gum and crisp packets. We got there in the nick of time, climbed aboard and slumped into the first available seat. An elderly man behind us said, "I reserved this seat."

After four hours of constant seat-changing, we arrived. Thrown around in a hubbub of passengers, Hope tripped, tumbling onto the concrete.

"Are you okay?" I was already on my knees, patting the innocent culprit. It licked my fingers, soaking them with drool.

"I'm alright," stuttered Hope as I checked the name tag.

"Her name is Joy! The perfect trio! Hope, Faith and Joy!" With no owner in sight, I lifted her into my arms.

Three monotonous hours later, we arrived. In anticipation, I tucked my unkempt locks behind my ears, as Hope twisted the door handle. Above us stood a cloaked figure peering down from the large oak staircase.

"Hope, Faith. I've been expecting you." As he gestured for us to follow him, my legs were wobbling like jelly and puddles flooded my forehead.

"How do you know who we are?" Hope asked.

"I know many things. I know you escaped the orphanage, snuck onto a train and stole a dog. My dog!" Joy leapt from my arms and scurried towards him. Hope and I looked at each other in shock; he'd been tracking us. "Seeing as you don't have enough money, I offer you this: transfer the disease from Faith to Hope with unknown consequences."

I couldn't stand the idea. My own sister, trading with me. We'd come to cure the disease, not transfer it.

"Deal." stated Hope. I tried to interject, but she'd decided. I embraced her and, as tears seeped down her shirt she whispered, "Always have Faith, Faith."

Ushered towards the purple curtain I waited inside. I couldn't stop myself. I peered back through the curtains and there she was: a pile of ashes.

"Time's up, pens down!" the teacher announced. I plopped my pen onto my desk and raised my paper into the air. I melodically tapped my ankles against the legs of my chair, thrilled with what I had written. Even though the test was over, Hope, Faith and Joy would remain with me forever.

The Letter

By Insha Dharamsi - age 12

It was over.

The earth had never felt so dead without my mother. The once emerald grass and vibrantly coloured flowers wilted. The round, ripe coconuts that fell from the towering trees were sour and rotten. Every day was the same grey, lifeless motion, like a doll revolving in a jewellery box. I went to grand buildings where 'helpful' adults would talk about my future. They 'understood what I had been through', but I knew they didn't.

Every night was dull, dark and filled with horror. Scenes of bombs falling replayed in my head alongside gunshots and blaring sirens echoing in the panic-filled city. I'd moved away from danger now, but sadness still followed me.

It was on a cold, Monday morning when I met Mrs Humes. She arrived in a mustard yellow car which seemed out of place in the atmosphere, the rain lashing furiously against the windows and grey clouds circling above us like a troop of soldiers preparing for battle. As I stared out of the foggy window, a head full of bouncy blonde curls popped out behind the car door followed by two small hands gloved in thick rainbow wool and a large pink coat, sheltering her from the rain. I assumed she was a teacher by the way she was dressed. The clang of the school gate rung through the hallway and the click clack of someone ascending the stairs. A few minutes later I was seated in a small, bright office, facing the strange lady .

"Hello, Olivia I'm Mrs Humes," she exclaimed. "It has been brought to my attention that you have been struggling with the war and the many scary memories that must come with it. I want to understand your thoughts and your feelings. Do you want to talk about it?"

This was uncomfortable. I wasn't ready to declare all my secrets to a woman I barely knew. Not yet. She was pushing too far, delving deep for the key to my mind. If I talked about the memories and sadness of the war she would laugh and say I was being dramatic. That's what everyone else did. I didn't want to stay here. Abruptly, I stood up and left, the door slamming shut with a loud thud leaving Mrs Humes alone.

The next morning, I woke up filled with the poisonous feeling of regret swirling around in my mind. That *one* buzzing fly hadn't drowned in the murky waters of my thoughts; it was getting louder and louder. So I decided to write a letter, filled with my thoughts, dreams and doubts, flowing from the cage with no key. It was sent to the one person I knew that would listen - Mrs Humes.

Just a week later, a large square envelope arrived on my doorstep, addressed to me! It was encouraging and thoughtful, telling me that I wasn't alone and that the right people would help and listen to any problem big and small. She would stand by me and we would get through it together.

Finally, someone had heard my pleas and was ready to help. Finally, I felt hopeful, that there was someone who cared about me.

The Magic of the Fairy Fruit

By Sandra Sarah - age 11

As you know, I am obsessed with fairies. I have always wished to become a fairy. I was once just an ordinary human being, going about my day-to-day life without any major changes or surprises. But one day, everything changed when I decided to try a new fruit that I had never tasted before. I'm still not quite sure what happened that day, but I know that my life has never been the same since then.

As I was strolling through the dense forest, I suddenly heard a strange noise that startled me: *RUMBLE!* After a moment of confusion, I realized that the sound was coming from my stomach, which was growling loudly. It was a clear indication that I had not eaten in quite some time and was feeling extremely hungry. The sensation was quite uncomfortable and I knew I had to find something to eat soon.

As I wandered in search of food, my eyes were drawn to a strange-looking fruit hanging from a nearby tree. I was hypnotized by the glowing fruit. Curiosity getting the better of me, I reached up and plucked the fruit from its branch. With a sense of anticipation, I took a bite and immediately felt a powerful sensation coursing through my body. It was as if a sudden burst of energy had been unleashed within me, leaving me feeling invigorated and alive. Despite this newfound vitality, I also noticed a growing sense of drowsiness creeping up on me. It was a strange and confusing experience, one that left me feeling both energized and drained at the same time. I slowly closed my eyes and found myself sound asleep, not moving a muscle.

As I slowly awakened, a strange sensation crept across my back, causing an intense itchiness. Reaching behind, I felt something soft and silky underneath my fingers, but I couldn't quite grasp what it was. I decided to quench my thirst by the nearby river and proceeded to walk towards it. As I bent down to drink some water, I caught a glimpse of my reflection on the water's surface. To my utter surprise, I saw that I had transformed into a fairy, complete with delicate wings and a shimmering aura. My mind was racing with disbelief and confusion - how could this even be possible? Am I a fairy? Where is my wand?

I can't believe what I'm experiencing right now. It feels like a dream, but it must be real. The sensation is so surreal, and I can't help but feel overjoyed. Being a fairy has always been a fantasy of mine, and now it's come true. I want to savour every moment of this magical experience. Can you imagine what it's like to be a fairy?

My hopes and dreams have come true!

A Sense of Hope

By Jiya Gadhia - age 13

Hannah stared at the picture lying in her hands, her eyes puffy and red. The concrete floor below her, disguised with a badly cut carpet, was hard and uncomfortable to sit on. Yet how could she complain, she was an orphan. That meant no one cared for your opinion. No one bothered to ask if you anything. Hannah put the photo down on the carpet, her grandmother's sympathetic smile gazing up at her. She wiped her tears away and sniffled. It was late at night – around 11ish. She swore that she was the only room with a light still on. Her only friend, Kiara, had recently been adopted, so Hannah was all alone. Again. She was used to being alone – her parents died in a fatal car crash when she was 5, and her paternal grandma took her in. That was until she passed away.

Hannah's grandma had always been sick. She was diagnosed with leukaemia a long time before Hannah was born, but wasn't too affected by it until her final few years. Hannah was alone when she was 5, and alone again now at 13. Life was going around in a full circle. And sadly, that circle went around far sooner than she expected. Hannah picked up the battered book on the floor, turning the page.

The familiar scent of her grandma swam through her nose. Hannah half-smiled as she remembered her passion for reading. This one was her favourite – a thrilling murder mystery.

She heard a scream. A blood-curdling, top of your lungs scream. Hannah's eyes shot straight up, and she could hear the small pitter-patter of footsteps outside the door. She shot up and ran towards it. The doorknob was cold to the touch, and she twisted it to see carnage outside. Other orphans popped their grubby heads around the doorframes, trying to understand whatever happened, and the caretakers were running up and down the dim hallway.

'Everyone, follow me,' one of them said, and all the children closed their doors chattering excitedly through the labyrinthine hallway.

The caretakers whispered as quietly as possible. Mrs Shah, the lady who ran the orphanage ran into the crowd.

'Everyone, calm down!' she exclaimed, as the police cars whipped round, their sirens blaring. She ran towards a police officer, Hannah secretly following.

'An incident happened,' said Mrs Shah. 'One of our caretakers is dead on the floor. The kids can't know, but is it safe here?'

Hannah could hear a gasp behind her, and turned to see Alex, a boy her age from the floor above her.

'No way, someone got murdered?' he whispered, his green eyes staring into Hannah's. Hannah stared at the detectives, who were writing notes down, and thought back to the book lying on her bedroom floor.

'You know what, I'm gonna help. I'm gonna investigate it,' and she smiled, for the first time in a while. 'For my grandma,' she muttered to herself, and a sense of hope swirled in her heart.

The Key

By Freya Menhinick - age 11

I stand still, frozen to the spot, transfixed by the sight in front of me. Tables are flipped, windows are shattered, lamps are broken, and the brand new sofa is awkwardly balancing on its side.

"Mum!"

No response.

"Mum!"

The house is silent. My heart is pounding in my ears. There's a note on the floor. I pick it up, my hands trembling, and read it.

If you want your mother back, meet at the Eiffel Tower, Friday 3pm. Bring the key.

And if you want to see her again come alone.

My mum gave me a key when I was little and told me to never give it to anyone. I wonder if I should give them the key.

I have to. For mum.

Tears stream down my face. I have no idea what to do. Friday is tomorrow and the Eiffel Tower is on the other side of town. I drop to my knees, head in my hands. I soon get up, remembering that crying doesn't help anything. I start pacing around the room thinking of ways to get to Champ de Mars. I could take the bus or a train? I'm almost out of ideas when I remember that Uncle Henry's got a shop on the square near the Eiffel Tower. I'll email the school on my mum's account and tell them that I'm going to be off school today with a cold. The plan all starts coming together. I just have to remember to wake up early so I can walk to my uncle's house in the morning.

The sun shines through my bedroom window and I'm up as quick as a flash. Butterflies flutter in my stomach for the day ahead. I pack snacks and drinks. I lock the door and follow the road to my uncle's. When I get there, I ring the doorbell and wait for an answer. Uncle opens the door with a great big warm smile on his face. He asks me what I'm doing and I tell him that Mum has a meeting all day and said I can come to work with him. He says, "Sure," and soon enough we're outside his shop window. It's 2:58, I should really be getting to the meeting point. I tell Uncle that I'm going to get a snack and a drink.

As I arrive at the Tower, I see a shadowy figure up above and I take the elevator to the top. Soon, in front of me, I see mum tied to a chair with rope. I gasp.

"Leah!" she cries.

"Mum!" I reply. I take a deep breath and slowly hand over the key from around my neck. I give it to the man and he pushes Mum to me. I untie her immediately and she holds me in the biggest hug in the world.

Hope

By Nikkita Karia - age 10

A shadow that lurks behind me, a shadow in my head. When they have my back, I don't know whether it is time for them to help. In my head they mutter, they speak to me of hope. When I am lost in my thoughts, and cruel comments fly around like the golden snitch lost on a Quidditch pitch, they remind me of happiness, and whisper of hope. When no one wants to talk, they force me to embrace hope. Despite the fact that they tell me of hope, I wonder to myself what is hope? Is it not just a feeling, or a wise word. Is it a cruel comment, or a fun exciting song they sing all day and night? I think of it as a treasure chest waiting to be unlocked, or a spirit coming to help comfort me and tell me stories .

But what if hope is a person? What if hope is a thing? What if hope is a monster who is trying to be mean? What if hope is the thing that makes you happy? What about all the joy not tears, forget about the worry of the words that they call you and think of finding your own new beginning. Think about the time they called you great, think about the time you were a hero, that was the time hope came to you. The time where you helped others, and when you gave them the story of hope. When you made just that little difference, when you helped, when you broke the mould, when you broke the bias, when you were the change.

I know I'm a little boy sitting in my room listening to my thoughts and responding in a nice way, breaking the bias and breaking the mould. I tell the people that no matter what age they are, hope lives deep inside them. I tell them all the good things about me that lifted me to success, I don't mention the bullies who were an insignificant part of my life, I just reiterate the feeling of hope as a power deep inside you. Hope is a feeling you can feel, hope is a word you can accomplish, but hope is your own, hope is your voice and hope is a word of power.

The past was the past and now is now. The hope that lives inside is still yet to be let out.

Even when it is the simplest thing or the hardest thing, the hope inside you is your burning fire that is never to be put out.

How hope was my success and how I thank the bullies who helped me take the path of success. They taught me to understand what hope was, and now I need to share my full story of how the bully made me stronger.

Even the worst can bring you to the strongest stage. Hope, happiness and joy are your most reliable. Forget all the rest.

Daisy, My Dying Dog

By Shanaya Bhalsod - age 11

Once there was a dog called Daisy, she was admired very much by her owner, Savannah. One very warm and bright day, Savannah took Daisy for a walk. Daisy hadn't been for a walk in what seemed like an eternity, but looked as tired as if she had already gone for three walks previously. Savannah took Daisy to the park but Daisy was walking slowly and sadly like she was depressed about everything in her life. Perturbed about Daisy's health, Savannah took her home and assumed Daisy was merely tired and hadn't got much sleep the previous night and needed rest. She took Daisy to bed and hoped everything would be normal the next day while she was at school.

Savannah woke up the next morning thinking about whether Daisy was still not feeling so well and went to get Daisy's favourite breakfast to make her feel better, but as she approached the dog bed, Daisy didn't run up to the food like she usually did. Instead she dozed off into a deep sleep. Although she felt anxious, Savannah went down the stairs and went to school.

Later, when she got back home, Daisy was still asleep, whining, and the day went on.

Getting even more anxious and afraid, Savannah called up the vet and booked an urgent appointment for later that day so they could figure out what was wrong.

Afraid and frightened, Savannah, her parents and Daisy got into the car, expecting the worst: they would have to put her to sleep! Worried, they got out of the car and walked to the entrance. They went inside and were instructed to sit down and wait for the vet to pick up the dog. Before long, the vet arrived and took Daisy to a special room to see what was happening in her body. They assumed it was a bug going around, but had never seen such a high temperature before of 41 degrees Celsius (the highest a dog can reach before dying). Whimpering, Daisy suddenly went cold to 17 degrees and kept bouncing back and forth like a tennis ball at Wimbledon

They got home, and all they could think about was what it would be like to lose their dearest companion, Daisy. No one knew it, but Daisy's health was reliant on them. Thinking that it was their last day together, Savannah decided to spend more time with Daisy. She gave her even more affection, love and attention than she normally would. To her surprise, Daisy seemed a little better the next day. Each proceeding day, Daisy grew more and more well.

On the fifth day after the family had first brought Daisy home from the vet, they took her back to be examined as she looked so much better. The vets realised that Daisy had just been feeling down and lonely and that the antidote was a lot of love, quality time with family and their attention.

Love really is the best medicine!

Alive, or Not?

By Fatima Khakoo - age 13

I didn't think the house was actually haunted until I noticed a trail of blood, leading to the window in the corner of the bleak, cold and dark room. I could smell the decay and the feeling of dampness in the atmosphere. The smell of death lingered in the air.

Emily had disappeared!

Emily and I had entered an ancient town made of warren tunnels and narrow, twisting alleyways. Initially, I felt a bit anxious and panicked as I realised that we were completely disoriented. The unfamiliar surroundings made it even more difficult, and I was alarmed. Soon we arrived at a ghostly area with a deserted castle crawling with mould and damp, with gaping windows like haunted eyes staring at us. We looked up and saw a veil of dark black smoke and towering chimneys. The bright full moon was drowned in heavy clouds, and we could hear the raven shriek.

As we got out of the car, we noticed the rotting rubbish and broken glass that lined the big metal gate. A heavy steel chain was wrapped over it, ensuring no one got in.

However, we managed to fit through the bars!

The door opened to a long, dimly lit corridor and right in front of us was a flight of stairs leading up. The spiral stairs twisted and turned sharply, changing direction at every corner.

"Hello?" I shouted, my voice echoing eerily. We entered a big, dusty, bare room. This was a place of shadows and whispers! A chill shivered down my spine as I watched Emily looking inside an old, broken table, sitting in the corner of the room. The dull light had bodies of dead flies hanging from it and as I looked back to see what Emily was doing, all I could see was drops of blood leading to the crumbling window.

Forty-eight hours later, Emily still hadn't been found. The senior detective, Carlos, walked up to me, and I pressed my quivering lips together, trying to hold my smile, but my chin started to tremble, and tears welled up in my eyes. He told me Emily had been murdered!

Yet, I remained obstinately certain it was not true. I held hope that Emily was alive, being kept hostage against her will.

Over the next few days, Carlos remained in contact with me informing me that the case was almost over. They had stopped prioritising finding Emily, and I almost ran out of hope. Soon after, the verdict stated Emily had been murdered after being attacked in the castle, but by what, no one knew. Despite this, I remained hopeful that Emily was alive.

Two weeks later, I was back at school, focusing on my GCSEs, and every night I remembered Emily. Then, one night, at midnight, I received a life-changing text message from an unknown number. At first, I thought it was a trick, but it read,

Hi, it's Emily, I'm coming home. I'm alive and safe.

The Emerald

By Sia Kapur - age 9

"Hi everyone," I said.

"Hi, so what do you want to do?" Lexi replied.

"Well we could watch a movie," I suggested.

"Yeh," screamed Zahra.

We all walked into the lounge and I realised my photo was out of place. As soon as I touched it the ground opened up and we fell down down down!

Everything was black. I saw a flash of light at the end of the tunnel. I blinked a few times, then I opened my eyes and saw a blur of three faces. I rubbed my eyes using my sleeve then I realised it was Lexi, Zaynab and Zahra peering over me blocking the blinding sunlight. I stood up, confused, where were we?

When I looked around I saw a lot of candy. It was an incredible sight: lollipop trees, caramel mountains and cotton candy clouds.

Eventually, we came across a strange creature, something we had seen before, but it was much bigger and it was alive. It was a ... gummy bear! He was pushing a cart of peppermint sticks down the road.

"Are you seeing this?" Zaynab whispered, as she nudged me.

"If you're seeing a walking gummy bear then I am," I replied. I walked up to the gummy bear and said, "Excuse me, but where are we and who are you?"

"We are in Candyland and I am Ami the gummy bear," said Ami. "Who and what are you?"

"I'm Zahra, she's Lexi, she's Sia and she's Zaynab and we are humans," Zahra blurted out.

The gummy bear asked, "What brings you here?"

Everyone was silent.

"We fell from the sky," I said. "And we need to get home."

"Oh, you need to find the emerald stone. Here's a map to get there. Once you get the stone, show it to the sun. Take this peppermint stick, you will need it to slay the dragon," the gummy bear said as he handed me the map and Zaynab the peppermint stick.

"Thank you for your help," Zaynab said.

"We'd better get going," Lexi said. "Bye, gummy bear."

We set off and figured out the way into the forest. Eventually, we came across a huge castle with a dragon guarding it. I hoped we would get home safely.

Remembering what Ami had said, I grabbed the peppermint stick from Zaynab. Suddenly, the dragon spotted me with its beady eyes. It plunged down from the castle. Zaynab and Zahra distracted the dragon, while Lexi pushed me up onto it. I shoved the peppermint stick into the dragon's back, then it dropped to the ground, defeated.

As we stepped inside the castle, I saw the emerald on a pillow in the middle of the room. We ran to the stone, grabbed it, showed it to the sun and landed back in the lounge. Everyone stood there silent.

Then I said, "So you still want to watch that movie?"

We all burst out laughing.

Etiquette

By Zoya Pope - age 10

There once was a girl called Alex who lived in Dublin. Her parents died when she was a toddler, but she wasn't thinking about the past, she was more concerned about the future.

Especially today.

Today was the day her life was going to change. Since the age of three, Alex had been an orphan, but one day, the matron at the orphanage told her she was going to be adopted. Alex was ecstatic. She couldn't believe it, someone actually wanted her!

The next day Alex was eager to hop on the train, she couldn't stop smiling. This was it, her ticket to freedom! The Einsteins were a fancy family of three: the mother named Diana, her husband, Albert and their child, Jerry. They were very posh, the kind of people who call dinner, 'supper', and drink with their pinky finger out.

Meanwhile, Alex was the total opposite. She chewed with her mouth open and ate with her hands. They didn't get much food at the orphanage, and when they did, she always ate the leftovers.

As Alex got off the train, she saw the shadow of a person underneath a beautiful hazel tree next to a posh car. It was Albert.

"Hi!" Alex exclaimed.

"Good morning," replied Albert. "I suppose we must get home then."

When they got home, Alex met Diana and Jerry who didn't fancy the look of her. Dinner was very awkward. Whilst the Einsteins were eating the tiniest pieces of food ever, Alex was stuffing herself as if she'd never eaten in her life.

Diana exclaimed, "Now now dear, there's no rush!"

Later, at the dinner table, Diana said she had a surprise for Alex, took her upstairs and held out a book in her face.

"Erm... Mrs Einstein," Alex muttered. "I'm dreadfully sorry, but I can't read, they didn't teach me in the orphanage." "Well darling," replied Mr Einstein. "We'll have to work on that, but for now I shall just tell you that this book is called, 'Everyday Etiquette'."

"Is erm.. ertiqute why you're so fancy?" asked Alex.

"Why, it's normal," said Diana.

For the next few days, Mrs Einstein (very strictly) taught Alex everything about etiquette. It was very hard, but she believed she'd tried everything and frankly done quite well. Even though she thought she had improved Alex, made her better, she was very wrong indeed.

Mrs Einstein looked outside at all the other girls playing and having fun, then looked at her own child. Miserable. Diana went to apologise. "Alex, dear, sorry for trying to change you. I just want to tell you that you never have to try to fit in, because everyone is lucky just to have you being - well, you."

"Really? Do you mean it? Oh thank you so much Mrs Einstein," Alex cried.

"Alex dearie, you can call me Diana." And from then on, Alex was accepted, just for who she was.

Blood, Mud, Sweat and Tears

By Ralph Warne - age 10

It's the lead up to the biggest rugby game of the season. Ralph and his brother George are playing and hope to win. Saracens play Northampton Saints who are unbeaten.

It's a promising week building up to it. Owen Farrell's kicking is good and so are Maro Itoje's carries. Elliot Daly looks brilliant as always and so do Ralph and George. The manager's looking forward to it, as he is really impressed. Everything is going swimmingly, until something terrible happens. It is revealed that Northampton are paying the referees and cheating!. Marco Riccioni is fuming and says that it's annoying.

"But it'll be alright as we are Saries!" he says.

Five days later, Saracens arrive at the Stone X Stadium and they get ready for the warm up, and Owen Farrell gets ready to deliver the team talk.

"I know they've been cheating," he says. "But we can rise above it with mental power and mental strength, physical strength and physical power. Saracens rugby is what beats cheats. Saries on three: one, two, three, Saries!"

The game gets underway and immediately Northampton are on the attack. Maro Itoje gets sent to the shops and back. Everyone thinks they are going to score but, boom, Elliot Daly is there and wins Saracens a lineout. Saracens lose the lineout and Northampton kick to gain ground and they have a great kick chase. Elliot Daly spills it and the Saints win it back to then go on to score a try. This reign of terror continues until half time, when the score is Saracens 3-33 Northampton.

Owen Farrell brings everyone in for the team talk.

"If I'm gonna be honest, we've been terrible these first forty minutes. They want this premiership title more than us, they *have* been better than us. But what I want you to do when we get back on that pitch, want it more, embrace the feeling of being able to win the league, think of what you could be if we beat them today. Feel the pitch, the fans, the players and most importantly, victory. Saries on three: one, two, three, Saries!"

They go out for the second half. Saracens stop Northampton from scoring points and instead Saracens score at the other end. Drop goals, tries, penalties and all that jazz.

It's the last minute and the score is 30-33 to Northampton. Saracens are in their eighth phase. They have a quick line break, Ralph is through, he's just got the fullback to beat. He slices a grubber past the fullback. He picks it up and puts it down to score the winning try. Owen Farrell scores the conversion and the Saries have won.

Now they can hope to win the league.

The Strange Wooden Door

By Tianna Nathwani - age 8

In a land far away, there were two children named Belle and Ben who were both 10 years old. They were the luckiest children on earth because they lived in the Land of Candy.

Candyland is the only place on this earth that is truly magical, a place full of sweet treats. There is a chocolate river with marshmallows, lollipop trees, sugar and cotton candy clouds. It is always warm and has a big rainbow every day to cheer you up.

Ben and Belle loved living in Candyland, but they both were always uncertain by a strange looking wooden door that they saw every day.

One day Ben and Belle's friend said to them, "Do you mind going through that door and fetching a treasure chest?"

"Sure" said Ben confidently.

"I don't think so, what if we get lost or something?" said Belle.

"Of course we won't get lost, you're 10 years old and you're telling me you're afraid of going through a door and fetching a treasure chest?"

“I guess you’re right, let’s go.”

They walked up to the door and turned the handle curiously to see what was inside. When they opened the door, they found a deep dark forest. It was cold and creepy, yet they decided to keep walking. Then they came across a house full of sweets and chocolates. “How about we ring the doorbell and ask if they have the treasure chest?” They rang the doorbell and waited for it to open. The door creaked open and they walked inside.

The door slammed behind them, making it go pitch black. In the distance they saw a green misty light and they followed it. Out of nowhere a little pixie called Develin jumped out in front of them. “Hello children would you like some food, said Develin very sweetly.

“Yes please,” said the children. They followed her into a room. “Wait here and I’ll be back,” said Develin.

The children waited for hours and finally she came back with a bright red button in her hand and asked the children to press the button on the count of three. “One, two, three!" The button beeped so loudly that the ground shook like an earthquake. The children shut their eyes.

When they opened their eyes, they had no way of getting out, they were trapped! “Hey let us out” the children shouted.

“Wait” said Belle. “Look there is the treasure chest!

"You’re not having that treasure chest, because it's for me to use," said the pixie”, and she left.

Ben said, “If we are quick, we could free ourselves and grab the chest and run back home.” So, they freed themselves, grabbed the treasure chest and ran as fast as they could all the way back home.

"But I will be back to get you someday!" screamed Develin slamming the door behind her!

So, Belle and Ben were safe and happy once again.

Beneath the Darkness

By Ruby Neale - Age 13

Tears of rain descend as the wind screams and the trees quiver in fear.

Tonight marks exactly three years since I first laid eyes on her.

Three years since I first caught a glimpse of her soft glow as she danced throughout the night. Three years since my heart has ached for her presence every night, yearning to see her flowing beautifully across the corridor as she dances wildly. Even the darkness is captivated by the way she moves, by the way she manages to emit the brightest light whilst being overshadowed by a cover of pitch dark.

Tonight is different however. Tonight, she seems weaker, worn down by time and conflict. Tonight she does not dance, instead she meanders slowly and leaves small trails of tears behind her to dry and cease into nothingness. Watching her weep feels wrong, it feels immoral and cruel. So tonight, for the first time, I am going to talk to her. Except I cannot walk, my feet are rooted in place, my breath is hitched and my breathing in a strange rhythm. Standing here is not going to get me to her though, I cannot bear to see her like this, depleted of her glow and charm. She is merely a hollow shell of herself. There in the darkness that bears the weight of a thousand tortured cries and suffocating souls, I decide that I cannot watch the woman who brings light to the heaviest of nights, who has the power to persuade even the most stubborn of men with her smile, the woman who keeps the Earth turning on-kilter, suffer in the most horrific way. There, in the opaqueness of the night, I reach down and drag my legs forward, I open my eyes a little wider, I stand a fraction taller and I stride over towards her.

A cold gaze meets mine and my heart stops, she wipes her tears and returns her gaze to the floor.

"Hello." Her head is hung low as she utters that single word. My lungs have to inhale to make sure that I don't perish right then and there. She lifts her head again to meet my piercing stare and smiles weakly, she has lived many lives, each one wearing her down more than the last. Reaching my hand out into the impenetrable darkness, I utter the only words I can think of as she takes both my hands.

"Hello."

That eases a soft chuckle out of her and it is the only sound I wish to ever hear again. In the gloomy, inky room I can see her up close, I can recognise every emotion, I can sense her by how she breathes alone, I can hear every thought and adore every second of it. The darkness is banished by light as every speck of passion returns to her glowing flame again. Everyone watches in awe, they are all disbelievingly starstruck as she is ablaze with an alluring spirit.

Christmas Hope

By Avni Desai - Age 12

Early one Saturday morning, Alex came down to see his mum, dad and two older sisters sitting around the dining table. All of them were suspiciously quiet. Alex slowly walked around, looking confused.

He awkwardly said, 'Good morning, guys'. They all just nodded. After some time, he asked, 'Okay, what happened?' because he knew something wasn't right.

One of his older sisters said, 'Let's talk outside.' They both walked out.

His sister began, 'You see, Aunt May was in a car crash and now she's in hospital. Doctors are saying that she might not survive. They are doing everything they can, but cannot promise survival.'

Alex was stunned and didn't know what to say, so he just began crying, because he couldn't say anything. His sister just began hugging him and calming him down. He was devastated.

A few weeks later, they visited Aunt May in the hospital. There were some signs of survival chances. They didn't know if their lives would ever return to normal. Over time she was slowly getting better, but nobody except Alex believed she would get better.

Only Alex had hope.

The family thought that it was best to turn Aunt May's life support off, as they thought she wouldn't live, but Alex and his sisters managed to persuade them not to.

The doctors would tell them that May couldn't live, but they had faith in their children and told them to let May live a little longer. She had so much left to do that she couldn't go yet.

It was Christmas Day, December 25th. They received a call saying that Aunt May was going to live. Everyone was so relieved and happy that Alex and his sisters had persuaded them to keep hoping. Only the three siblings had hope.

There is always hope at Christmas.

The Power of Hope

By Suri Khurana - age 13

Hope gives one positivity and a desire for something; everyone deserves hope. The small Ivywood Village in North England was fortunate to have Asha in house 22, for she practically impersonated hope.

Recognising everybody's dilemmas, she could give guidance to an adult to make the most of the world and later comfort a bawling child. Perhaps she was a plaster for others' insecurities. Nonetheless, as time went by, Asha's fame for decision-making spread and soon she couldn't bear the weight of others' responsibilities.

Some days she felt unsure whether her advice was correct, but the gratitude she received overshadowed the negativity, and Asha soon helped others, relying on their praise for motivation.

On a particularly sunny day, a small boy approached Asha, tears streaming down his bright red cheeks. The boy sniffled before whispering, "My friend, he told me to go away, I feel sad". Laughing sympathetically, Asha knelt beside him, using her sleeve to wipe the heavy tears that poured from his eyes. "Perhaps he's having a bad day, give your friend some space and continue being kind!" The boy managed to creep a smile upon his face before running off happily.

When Asha came into school, she was a pillar of support for all her classmates. She helped a boy take care of his sick mother by giving advice and pitching in for the medicine. Another day, Asha guided a sixth former who was stressed due to exams. Asha reassured her and offered to collect the textbook she needed.

During the week, the "School Rebel" was in jeopardy of being expelled. Once again Asha found it her position to suggest making amends with others and helping out where possible. She felt proud when helping others.

But the next week everything took an unfortunate twist. When the boy's mother passed away, she was blamed. When she found out the sixth former had failed her exam due to Asha bringing the wrong book, Asha was devastated. To make matters worse, her advice to the rebel had done nothing but persuade the school that he meant trouble and there was no doubt of expulsion. Asha persuaded herself that she was unsuitable to help others anymore.

The following evening, Asha was soon brought back to her senses due to an unexpected visit from her Nani, and was reminded harshly from her, "*Bheta*, you act like the weight of the world is on your shoulders, it's not! *You're thirteen!*

"You have supported these people, but remember the outcome is not your fault." Asha smiled. "My love, in Hindi, Asha means Hope," whispered Nani, before hobbling out of the room.

That coming week, Nani's words remained in her head. To her surprise, Asha was thanked for her efforts and her classmates could see positivity in the outcome. As for Asha, she learnt not to live on the positive affirmations from others, but to live with her own self-confidence and to know that there is always *hope*.

The Forest Prince

By Carys Senior - age 9

My name is Luca, Luca Maxwell. My mum disappeared one night when I was three. She was the best mum, and I didn't know how to go on without her. I would make up stories about where she had gone and why she couldn't come home. My dad always hesitated when I brought her up because it made him sad.

My mum left me a music box and deep down I always knew that one day I would find her...

"Luca, breakfast!" shouted my dad from the stairs, one morning.

"Coming," I replied. I sat at the table. "Dad... can you tell me more about mum?" I asked.

"Oh Luca, not today," he looked sheepish.

"Please Dad, I want to know more about her," I begged.

"No!" my dad snapped. I stomped upstairs, got out my music box and started playing it, because it always seems to relax me. All of a sudden, I saw a fold just behind the mirror of the music box.

"What's this?" I pulled the flap further. It had a map showing where we lived, and a route leading to the forest. In my mum's handwriting it said, *Come and find me, it's your destiny.*

I knew I had to follow this map and, for the first time, I had an actual clue that could lead to my mum. I packed my bag and snuck out, making my way towards the forest. I walked the worn paths of the forest and, all of a sudden, an animal started to growl at me in the bushes. It jumped towards me, and before I could block myself, he stopped and stared at my music box, poking out of my pocket.

"Where did you get that?" asked the wolf.

"My mum gave it to me," I said, in disbelief and all of a sudden, he bowed to me.

"Let me take you to your Mum, Queen of the forest. She has been waiting for you," said the wolf. I got on his back, and he took me deeper into the forest. After a while we came to a stop.

"This is it," the wolf said, slipping me off his back. It was a castle, covered in vines, leaves, and all sorts of nature material on it.

"Son!" a lady in a fancy leaf dress came running towards me.

"Mum...?" She hugged me, I knew this was her, as hugs were something I could never forget."

"Why did you leave, and where are we?" I said, searching her face for answers.

"One question at a time! I had to come back to my kingdom. We could only be a family again if you were brave and found your way to me." She gave me a crown and smiled.

"Welcome home, Forest Prince. Your father is on his way, and we will be a family again," said Mum, with a warm smile.

"I hoped for this every day, and now it has finally come true," I said.

And that is the story of the forest prince.

Secret Power

By Liya Patel - age 11

I never knew this would ever happen. Flying, can you believe that?

I'm Juliet and I love exploring the jungle that lies ahead. I never knew I would find this place. The mystical caves enter the wishing pond. I had been walking for ages, sweat clinging onto my forehead as I wiped it away with exhaustion. I suddenly dropped my rucksack on the floor. *Water!*

After walking for hours, I nearly cried in relief that I'd found water. I rushed towards it all the exhaustion building up, the adrenaline inside me bubbling furiously. But I didn't realize that the water I drank was the water from the wishing pond. My wings didn't come fast.

I finally wanted to go home, but I had to walk another ten miles to get back home to my stepmum. You might know stepmums as kind and nice, but my stepmum was the complete opposite. If I did not eat like a princess, dress like a princess, or be a princess I would get told off. *Badly*. I sighed, getting ready to go home, dragging my aching feet, full of blisters, down the muddy tracks that led towards my *'home.'* I ran my hands through my knotted hair, trying to get rid of the knots that frizzed up my hair.

My stepmum was a very loved person in my village, but no one truly knew her *except me*. I knew she *hated* me. I knew that if I did one bad thing, I would get whacked on my hands again. I sighed as I looked at my hands, red and raw, scarred for life. Suddenly, my back started to hurt. I groaned in pain as I turned around stretching it. I squealed.

No! I have wings.

I squealed again. Finally, wings to carry me home. Sparkles surrounded me with excitement. The wings started to flutter, carrying me up to the sky. I shouted happily as I landed in front of my house. I hoped I would never see my stepmother again, but she was standing there, hands crossed and a stern look moulding her face. She was holding a stick.

Suddenly, *a blue glow filled my hands. It shot in front of me leaving my eyes to see* my stepmother dead on the floor.

No!

All the colour drained out of me, leaving me pale. I did hate her, but not that much so she died because of me.

She was the only person I knew. And I had killed her. My mind went fuzzy almost dizzy.

I felt anger, as she left me with nothing.

I felt guilty that I had killed her. I didn't mean to. But had I wished to?

The wishing pond that I had tried to find. My hope is to forget this ever happened. I will wish for my stepmother to come alive.

But a mixture of darkness and magic swelled in my heart, desperate to come out.

What will I do?

Which side should I choose?

Good or Evil?

Ninjas Forever, Cats Together

By Harley Hodson - age 11

Boom!

"What was that?" asked Sooty. Tabby suggested it could be a meteor that fell from the sky. Kira explained that it could be an explosion, but Roosty knew it had to be a crash of some sort.

The four cats all agreed to investigate and got into the ninja car. When they found the source of the explosion, they jumped out of the car and realized it was a bomb that had started a fire. Tabby's beige and orange stripy fur lifted because, all of a sudden, Marmalade, the evil bear, ambushed. He grabbed Tabby and jumped into a deep pit with the kidnapped cat. When Sooty realized what had happened, he screamed, "Follow that bear!"

The three remaining cats used their kicking ninja skills to get to the bottom of the pit and once they reached the bottom, they saw a closed door. Passing through the door, they found a dinosaur standing right in front of them! Kira was so frightened, his grey fur was shaking and he started miaowing.

The T-Rex roared proudly, before he chased his next lunch across the room. The ninjas thought there must be another room, but none of them had any clue as to where it could be. Sooty's white patch on his tummy sprang out in excitement.

"The next door is on the ceiling!" he exclaimed. But even with their high ninja jumps, they could never make it that high. Roosty had a great idea. They could run up the T-Rex's back and up to the door. Roosty's risky plan worked, and once they entered the next room, the cats saw lava and several pathways leading to another door. All of the pathways seemed like they were going to sink into the lava but one of them had to be safe. While the other two cats argued over which path they should pick, Sooty noticed that the third pathway had the symbol of a bear on it, so they decided to choose that path. Sooty let out a deep breath and stepped onto the path. It was safe, so they all crossed and opened the final door.

Marmalade's claws shone in the sunlight, while his red eyes stared deep into Sooty's soul. Tabby was sitting in a heavy cage near a fire. "Help me," she whispered to Kira.

Kira winked at Tabby and ran to the iron bars of her cage, using his ninja strength to break open the bars. Tabby was free, but Marmalade was furious! He punched Kira and Roosty right in the face so that they were knocked out! Then he grabbed Tabby and threw her out of the window! It was up to Sooty to beat Marmalade.

"Marmalade, why are you always so angry?" he said.

"I always hoped to be a ninja, but I'm a bear," said Marmalade.

"That's okay," said Sooty. "I can teach you some special skills that bears can do."

Marmalade agreed and after the other cats recovered, they all became friends.

Wish, and the Power of Hope

By Shaan Bachada - age 9

One day, lying on my bed, I was mourning over the event that happened five years ago:

I was jittery with excitement, it was the day I received my power. You see, the Igrades are not an ordinary family, we are a magical family! 'Wish!' my mother called. Hopping out, I was dressed wonderfully. I hastily ran to the magic stone. As I pressed it, nothing happened. I pressed it again. Nothing. Then I realised it was because I had no power.

Suddenly a tap on the window brought me out of my flashback. As I peeked out, to my surprise, I saw a strange creature which had webbed feet and feathers. However, its arms were that of a bear and under the feathers it had a heavily armoured torso. Just staring at it I felt my jaw hanging open. I don't know why, but it was as if my eyes were glued to it. Then I heard a scream from my sister's room. Amery came fleeing from her room with two more monsters chasing her. Suddenly one spat a green liquid at her dress. She turned and assaulted the creatures with plants. One withered in grapevines, the other turned to flee, but found my brother, Fiy's feet. He let rip several roars and a lion appeared, tore apart the monster and leapt away.

"Summoned him," said Fiy, casually. "From Rome Zoo."

Then my dad entered. "What have I said about *borrowing* from the zoo?"

"Why do you always eavesdrop?" Fiy cried back.

"It's not my fault my power is that I can hear really well," he sneered back.

"There is something bigger to worry about..." I broke in.

"Exactly," cut in Amery. "Those things ruined my dress."

With a sigh, I slipped out of the house. On my way to school, after the excitement of the morning, I spotted a few awe-struck children staring and pointing at me, making hushed comments, but thought nothing of it. When I got to school the classroom was filled with them...I mean those disgusting creatures. But on my way back to the house I saw that the whole of Rome was infested with them and on the evening news I discovered they were all over the whole of Italy, that is, except Naples and that was where we were heading...

When we reached Naples, we saw the monsters destroying it. *How are they able to defeat everyone so easily?* I wondered.

As if reading my mind, Dad said, "Be careful of their poisonous spit. Luck is the only reason Amery survived."

On that note, we went right in front of their next destination to trample: a barren field. Within seconds I was the only one standing out of my family. In my head, a voice roared, telling me not to give up. Soon I was tearing down enemies like they were paper. In seconds I'd defeated the whole army. It was at that moment I realised my power.

It was hope.

The Light Inside

By Isla Boyd - age 10

Despair. I wake up to it every morning. A swirling cloud that envelops me, sucking up any hope I might have had left. This morning was no different as I sloped down the stairs and collapsed into my chair, which creaked in protest. I was small and very skinny, with thin, mousy brown hair that hung limply by my shoulders. Devoid of any beauty it might have once had, a face that was sucked of expression and colour. Drab top and bottoms and greeny-brown, falling-apart trainers that used to be white. Today would be my last day in this horrific place, for tonight I was making my escape - to seek the thing that, finally, would make me whole again: Hope.

That night, I crept down the creak-ridden stairs, my feet silent and fast. My only resolve, the need to get out of the wretched orphanage. I remembered the day I was brought to this grizzly, grey building and loathed it so strongly it fuelled me to push on and prepare for this moment.

"No, I couldn't give up," I decided.

With those thoughts embedded in my mind, I strode on. Finally, I was at the entrance, a few steps away from the sweet taste of freedom.

Thump, thump, thump. My blood ran cold. It was the sound of Mrs Gabtar's boots as she gave chase to orphans attempting a leap of freedom. THUMP, THUMP, THUMP. She was gaining on me. I did the only thing I could. I ran until my feet were a lake of blisters and my trainers were reduced to shreds. Finally, able to relax, I lay down on the grass and fell into a deep sleep.

I woke to see daylight, blinding me after the night's gloomy adventures. I stood, knowing where I must go next. But it would bring back my pain, my hurt, my grief, like moths drawn to a flame. For this was the graveyard, my parents' final resting place. That morning I trekked through country paths that snaked their way across the landscape until I reached my feared destination. There it was - dark and foreboding.

Now was my final chance to turn back, but this was my only opportunity and I wasn't going to throw it away. So I stepped through...

Marble and crumbling rock tombs surrounded me, filling the air with the aroma of loss. Grief came back to me, fresh and hurtful as ever, like stabbing an old wound. My body crumpled, finally giving way to the overbearing weight of sorrow. But I stumbled on. By the time I reached their grave, my throat was sore from the piercing torrent of wails echoing through the abyss. My heart split open, and there it was. The answer I'd been searching for, etched in the polished marble:

"Hope is always with you".

It was. I felt it rushing up my body like a flood of golden ichor and harmony entwined.

My light inside.

Discovery

By Beatrix Gardner - age 8

This is a bit awkward, you are probably a human, but I'm a rat. Before you hold your nose, slam this book and run away, I want to tell you about my dream: I want to be an archaeologist.

My best friend, Cleopatra, is a mouse and she thinks we can't possibly get that job, but I think we can. Let me introduce myself: my name is Maria, I live in London, I have beige fur and lots of whiskers and I despise vipers.

Here's where the story starts:

I was trying to help Cleo find places for our first discovery and we almost lost hope until I found Lyme Regis. A girl called Mary Anning found lots of fossils there and she was only twelve. We needed to get there, but we needed someone to help us with directions. Cleo said she knew of someone that could help.

"It's going to be tricky getting past all these humans because we are rodents," explained Cleo. So I checked there weren't any vehicles, grabbed her tail and we dashed across the road into the zoo and I followed her to the enclosure.

There were lots of glass windows, with logs, twigs and some decorations. The humans saw me, held their noses and started running, giving us the place to ourselves. Inside the glass were lots of venomous snakes. That's right, Cleo was talking about a viper.

"Hello, my name isss Sssam, who are you?" questioned the viper.

"Hi Sam, I'm Cleopatra and this is my friend Maria! We need your help Sam, we are trying to find Lyme Regis, because we want to be archaeologists and make a great discovery!"

"Rodentssss? Archaeologissstsss? That sssoundsss ridiculoussss, but I do want to sssee Lyme Regisss again. Very well, usssssseee your clawssss to take apart the glassss and I will show you the way."

Sam was soon slithering along with us. As soon as we got onto the road, Sam led us down into the sewers which were dark, slimy and full of wee! We travelled for three days, until Sam told us we were there.

The beach was filled with stones, kelp and dried grass. There were people there, but they saw me and ran away screaming, holding their noses. We began digging. Cleo and I used our sharp claws to scratch around the rocks and dig deeper, and Sam used his tail to push the rocks around. We were digging for hours and every time someone shouted, "I've found something!" it was either a chocolate wrapper or a mouldy banana.

But then Cleo found something. I thought it would be another mouldy banana, but it was different. It was brown, with darker stripes and lots of bumps.

"I think it's a mammoth tooth," I said joyfully.

Thank you for not holding your nose, slamming this book and running away, but for reading about my dream and how we showed that even hopeful rodents can be archaeologists.

Teamwork Makes the Dream Work

By Maani Chauhan - age 11

"Riley, Iris, what do you want to be when you grow up?"

"We want to be interior designers!"

"Ah... interior designers? Why don't you become a doctor, like me and your mum?"

"Or an accountant like your older brother?"

"You don't believe in us?"

"Well, twins, interior design is a tough, useless job. Maybe stick to medical school. You could help many people!"

"So you don't believe in us? Wow. Great parents."

Riley and Iris - twin sisters who had parents with no faith in them at all...

After being stuck in a house with horrible parents together all their life and being miserable, they decided to go their separate ways. Both looked for jobs, but both failed, rejected for their dream job many times. They lost all hope...

Until...

Dear Diary,

I haven't seen Riley in so long. It's probably been around 3 years now.

I am being rejected for all the dream jobs I have applied for. I'm lost for hope... No one wants to accept me as an interior designer. What do I do? I may as well give up and become a doctor like Dad told me to, or an accountant like Mum said...

It's true, I'm useless...

Yours,

Iris

Then...

One day, when Iris was walking to another interview, with no hope left in her heart, she bumped into someone and dropped her files.

"Sorry about that," a familiar voice said. Iris looked into her eyes.

"Riley!"

"Iris!"

The twin sisters squeezed the air out of each other!

"What are you doing here?"

"Trying to pursue my dream and become an interior designer."

"Same!"

" But I'm miserably failing..."

"Same..."

"Hey I have an idea! What if we start our own interior design business? It will be a lot of work, but it will be worth it. I'm sure of it."

Iris thought about it. It would be hard, but that wouldn't matter if they worked together. So they started their own business, keeping one thing in mind: nothing and nobody could stop them. They opened a shop, they hired a team, and they did it - together. While the twins were growing their business, they came up with a quote. A quote that had a meaning: Teamwork Makes the Dream Work.

A few years later, the job was done. The business was thriving, and the twins were earning money. They lived happily and comfortably:

Riley was living in a 3 story house with her 2 cats, her husband and her 2 sons. As for Iris, she was living in a 2 story house with her husky, husband and daughter.

Dear Diary,

My life is so much better now. Riley and I finished our business and now we live our dream lives! We proved our parents wrong!

We created a quote too: Teamwork Makes the Dream Work.

Yours,

Iris

Lost in the Unknown

By Nakshatra Balaji - age 11

All around was black, only small pinpricks of light dotted the universe. Sometimes you were lucky enough to see the bright colours of the planets. Swerving through the galaxy was a contraption, out of control, bouncing rapidly through the unlimited space. Swooping and gliding, making the poor thing inside sick. It slowed down, but turned in the wrong direction towards...*The Earth!*

On the lush, green meadows, a brother and sister were playing cheerfully. Suddenly, the girl, Julia pointed up to the sky and said, "Look! There's something unusual!" She and George started running towards their small cottage and launched themselves through the door yelling, "Mum, come quickly!"

By now, the speedy, unknown object had crashed onto the meadows with a massive bang.

They sprinted towards the devastation, panting heavily. Whatever this vehicle was, it was massive. Shiny, metallic panels protected the interior and four thick legs for landing. Two of its legs were entirely damaged.

George screamed in fear and pointed at the door where a waxy-skinned arm hung. Gripping the sides, two bony fingers came first, then the rest. Looked intently at Julia and George, the creature had two antennae, sparkling yellow eyes, a green body and it was wearing a black jumpsuit with silver stripes.

Julia gasped "It's an alien!".

Everyone backed away, frightened. Slowly, he approached them and tried to communicate, but sensing the situation, began to operate his language translating gadget. The alien introduced himself as Ray and sadly mumbled that Spaceship 'Krang' had been damaged, its navigation chip corrupted, and all his hope of getting back home was drifting away. Julia consoled him and said he could stay with them until he found a way. The alien felt a pang of dismay as he trudged towards the cottage. He feared that he was stranded on Earth *forever*. For few days, Ray felt worried about whether he would ever reunite with his loved ones, hoped against hope that something would happen.

Ray's spirits lifted when he saw the children playing hide and seek outside. Ray turned invisible until, after some time, he revealed himself which sent them stumbling. Although he seemed relaxed, he still felt miserable inside. The following day, Ray visited Krang with little desire of fixing his spaceship. Memories flooded before him and a feeling of despair grabbed his heart. Suddenly, Ray was distracted by the appearance of a little object which he grabbed and gently opened. After looking inside, he jumped up in glee, excited to share the news with the family that he had found a spare navigation chip. Everyone was delighted.

Alien Ray worked hard to mend the spaceship with the help of the family. On the day of departure, Ray gave them the language translator as a token of appreciation. Then, with a heavy heart, Ray bid farewell and walked towards his spaceship. The engine started whirring before soaring through the air and disappearing.

George, always curious, typed 'Krang' on the translator, which brought smiles to everyone as they saw the word.

Krang means hope!

The Perplexing Escape From Home

By Misha Dekka - age 9

It was another boiling and strenuous day in the village. The sun was beaming at the two laborious children, as if it were signalling to them that these unfortunate, prolonged times would finally end.

Even though the village looked as if it was barren and bare, the lively noise of motorbikes and tuk-tuks and cars and bikes strewn over the broad road made it sound like a bustling city in New York!

The pathway, however, was a narrow route that was rocky and uneven. Only people who had hard and sturdy soles would have the strength to walk on that atrocity of a road.

The brothers, Chatur and Chakan, were going to the stream to get water. Surely, two miles is manageable for a nine-year-old child. That's what life was like in those parts. If you wanted your essentials to survive, you would have to achieve it. So, that is what they did. They worked for it.

The farm was a mass of land, with parts evenly divided into sections. Chatur and Chakan's family were growing tomatoes, aubergines, and jackfruit. These fruity delights would even be craved by the richest. The community stream was a narrow body of water that glowed a deep cyan by the land, but in the second-hand, onyx buckets, it was as clear as a cloudless sky. Both, Chatur and Chakan, sank the buckets into the stream, gently towed them out of the cooling, satisfying water and sluggishly trudged back home. In their brains, they were urging their muscles to quicken their pace, but the boys could not bear to do so.

"I cannot stand having to walk more than a mile or so, in the hot sun!" exclaimed Chakan, while grasping his bucket with both his hands, which was smothered in a sticky substance.

"Yes, I do agree with you, Chakan. And on top of that, it is exhausting and tiresome just walking around, with the sun's rays irritatingly beaming directly at our deeply tanned backs!" replied Chatur.

Just then, Chatur saw the silhouette of an unclear, blurry figure. He was not certainly sure if he should tell his brother that he'd seen something or keep it to himself. "Well, probably it was just a trick my eyes played on me," murmured Chatur.

"Chatur, did you say anything?" Chakan enquired.

"Um...Oh no, no, I did not say anything Chakan. It might have been the sun playing tricks on you," Chatur replied nervously, quite startled that he had been heard.

As the boys were talking, the same odd-looking figure came closer, even closer... The figure marched along towards Chatur and Chakan. The brothers kept on walking. Neither of them realised that "it" was heading for them.

Suddenly, Chatur noticed that the silhouette was a man, with a stooping shadow. He was dressed in a brown suit, which was pinned with uncountable metal badges. He also had a navy hat of the sort that a police officer would wear.

An Indian police officer.

Despair Woods

By Ariadni Filippidou - age 9

Calypso Hope was a girl who would never give up. That's what everyone had told her parents. But, in Despair Woods, Calypso wasn't so sure. Here, there was no sign of anything but suffering. Ever since the sorceress cast a spell on the forest, people had been trying to find the jewel that could release the woods from the spell. Every now and then, she came across sobbing people who cowered from invisible threats. Calypso wanted to join them. Letting herself drown in sorrow seemed... fulfilling. She could forget about what she had to do, about the people who were waiting to see if she came out.

But no. She had a job to do. To find the jewel that could release the woods from despair. She continued on her way, knowing the price she would have to pay.

Calypso walked further and further into the woods. A light shone through the trees. An ethereal light. She sighed. Words spun through her head; Despair, Hope, Sadness, Joy. Calypso continued to walk. She saw a woman with grey hair wandering around aimlessly. As Calypso neared, the woman noticed her and grabbed her arm.

"Find the jewel!" she yelled. Who was this woman? "Save me,save the woods!" she screamed. Then the woman blinked and the desperate look in her eyes disappeared. The woman turned and walked away from her. Calypso had the sudden urge to follow her and give in to despair.

Then, memories surged through her head. *Dad playing games with her. Mother hugging her. The townspeople cheering her name when she volunteered to save Despair Woods.* Calypso could not let them down. So, she continued.

The light that was visible through the branches began to brighten. Calypso ran forwards. Forwards through the dead branches. Forwards through the scraggly bushes. Forwards through the scrawny ivy. Forwards on the battered, broken ground. The light still shone. Brighter and brighter and brighter until Calypso skidded into a clearing. A jewel was on an altar made of twisted vines and black driftwood. Calypso walked forwards slowly. *Boom boom boom* went her feet. *Boom boom boom* went her heart. She reached out a shaking hand and touched the jewel. "Calypso," said a voice. "To save the woods requires a sacrifice." The words echoed in her head. "A sacrifice of what you value the most."

An image of her father went through her head. The voice laughed. Immediately, the woods began to change, but Calypso was running to her dad. Through the beautiful branches. Through the healthy bushes. Through the bright green ivy. On the strong, shining ground. She passed people who were smiling. Finally free of sadness and suffering. As she broke out of the wood she saw her father wheezing his last breaths. "Calypso." he said "You saved the woods." he smiled and breathed out for the last time. The Despair Woods were free. The price had been paid. She was free.

And in the laughs surrounding her, Calypso's sobs were lost.

I Wish I Was a Witch

By Eva Agarwal - age 9

Once upon a time, in a small pretty village in Hertfordshire, a little girl named Evelyn lived with her mum and dad. She was a big Harry Potter fan and always hoped of becoming a witch like Hermione. She always dreamt of receiving a letter from Hogwarts one day.

It was a cold, rainy Halloween evening and she dressed as Hermione with her wand in her hand. Evelyn merrily went out with her friend, April, for trick and treating. They collected a bucketful of their favourite candies, lollipops and chocolates and were happily walking back home, when all of a sudden there was a loud thunder clap. A flash of lighting struck Evelyn on her left shoulder. April panicked and ran to Evelyn's house shouting for help. Evelyn's parents came out running and quickly took her to the hospital. They asked April about what happened and once they heard the details, they saw a big hole in Evelyn's robe on her left shoulder. They all were astonished to see a Harry Potter Lighting bolt scar on her shoulder.

Doctors examined Evelyn and all her results came out normal. She soon became stable, but the last thing she remembered was when she was walking back home with April and there was loud thunder. She was discharged from the hospital at ten o'clock in the night. On their way back home, Evelyn asked her parents about her scar and whether April had got one too. Her mind started running in all directions, is this a sign that I'm a witch now? She even muttered a few spells to test her hope, but nothing happened, obviously.

By the time Evelyn took a bath, checked her scar for the hundredth time and talked to herself in the mirror like a witch, it was nearly midnight when she went to bed. She was asleep in seconds, but as the clock struck midnight, the official time for witch's hour, Evelyn had the most wonderful dream. She had made it to Hogwarts and everybody knew her name. She was the 'Girl who got the scar'. She woke up immediately, as this was always her dream and she always hoped to go to Hogwarts. Realising she was back in her room with muggle parents next door, she went back to sleep again, disappointed. In her dreams she was a witch again and this continued every night from that Halloween evening onwards when she was struck by the lightning.

Evelyn's hope of being a witch was answered in a unique way. She continued her Hogwarts journey every night as she slept, and led her muggle life during the day. Her best friend at Hogwarts was called 'Harmony' and obviously she was a Gryffindor, like her favourite, Hermione Granger.

Vines Entwined

By Jacob Healey - age 12

I had been stumbling blindly through the empty fields for what seemed like hours, and there had been no point. The dark lightning-streaked clouds above me had covered up all remains of hope. I had given up. The house wasn't there. But just as I was about to turn back... I saw it. There. It was just there. A warm light radiating through all this darkness. A light of hope. I squinted through my rain-peppered vision and could just make out what I had been searching for. The old house. Sure enough, there was Professor Galzagarrus beaming his familiar smile at me through the rounded windows.

As soon as I entered the cottage and hung up my rain-drenched coat, the comfortable warmth of the fire instantly enveloped me. I was safe now. What a relief it was to see the professor's eyes dance and flicker like fire itself after all these years. It had been so long, I had missed him so much. But there would be time for that later. I was too tired now.

Over the years, I had seen the wrinkles beneath his eyes slowly spreading, but now he looked different, much older, and I knew he didn't have much time left. But even in a million years, the fire in his eyes would never die. Never.

"You need rest, Clara," Galzagarrus told me firmly, sensing my weariness as I zoned in and out of reality.

That was probably true. I followed him as he led me to where I would sleep. Wishing me goodnight, he shuffled out of the room, leaving me alone. I collapsed onto the comfortable bed, completely exhausted.

The room was small and cosy, with a thick curtain separating me from the rest of the cottage. A dim candle cast its warmth and light off the walls. Intrigued, I sat up, as I noticed a thick book beside it. Back when I had a home I would always read for hours before I slept.

The book looked fairly interesting; the front cover was an intricate design of vines and other plants overlapping each other, fitting the title: *"Vines Entwined"*. Picking it up, I flicked through the torn and tattered pages, my eyes feasting upon the words, ravenously scanning through the pages, following the fascinating plot and concept of an alternative timeline, where plants would evolve to become the dominant species of Earth, swapping positions with humans. They would trap people with their long vines and slowly feast on their flesh. Just as we do to them.

I awoke with a start hours later, to realise I had fallen asleep, the book in my hand. As soon as my eyes came into focus I screamed. A long, emerald-green vine had emerged from within the very pages of the book, its shape writhing and contorting above me, staring straight at me, like a serpent ready to strike at its prey. Then it lunged straight at my neck and my screams stopped.

All hope had died.

How I Got A Best Friend

By Sophie Steele - age 10

My name is Melody Marine and I am 7 years old. I live at Aqua Rock in the north of the ocean. I am a mermaid with a blue tail and cyan hair. I'm very shy and I have no friends. One day, I hope I will find someone who gets me the way that my parents do.

A week later...

Today something unusual happened. A family moved into the old cottage at the end of my street. I saw a girl the same age as me, with her mum and a little sea puppy named Babo. The mum was pretty, with coral pink hair and striking blue eyes. The girl had a pink ombre tail and turquoise hair. Every child mermaid in the street crowded around Gemma except me. I just observed the crowd from my bedroom window.

I felt bad for Gemma; she had no room to settle into her new home. The mermaids on my street do not usually fuss so much, but Gemma had come from *Shimmer Lagoon.* If you have never heard of *Shimmer Lagoon*, it is a place just off the south of the ocean where all the most famous mermaids live. Gemma's mum was a super sea-model, but she wanted Gemma to have a normal childhood, so they moved here.

Lots of cameras surrounded Gemma and her house which made me angry. Could they not leave her alone? I looked around and spotted a big bush. Behind the bush was a tunnel which led to a big coral reef with rainbow coral. No one knew about it but me, so no one could harass Gemma if she came with me and stayed for a while. So I swam up to Gemma and said, "Would you like to follow me?" And she did.

I led her to the bush and we disappeared into the tunnel and through to the reef. It turned out that Gemma was into the same things as me! We talked for ages. Then I had an idea, I had always wished to have a best friend, so maybe I could try to be Gemma's. But before I could ask Gemma to be my best friend, she asked me! And I said *yes!*

A week later...

Gemma is my BFF (Best Friend Forever), and everything feels so much better knowing that I have someone to play with and someone my own age who I can talk to. Everyone has stopped crowding around Gemma and there are no more cameras. My mum always says, "*You hope, you dream and you achieve.*"

And that is how I got a best friend.

The Phoenix's Flight

By Kiara Shah - age 13

In the realm of Eldoria, where magic was as common as air and danger lurked in every shadow, Blair, a determined mage, and Kai, a valiant swordsman, embarked on a perilous quest. Eldoia, once a beacon of light, now lay in ruins, consumed by the spiteful flames of the Shadow Phoenix, a creature of darkness that threatened to devour all in its path. But a glimmer of hope remained - a legendary Phoenix's Feather is said to hold the power to vanquish the Shadow Phoenix and restore prosperity.

With determination burning in their hearts, Blair and Kai ventured into the desolate wasteland known as Ashen Plains. The air was thick with the acrid scent of smoke and the ground was scorched black by the Shadow Phoenix's flames. Every step taken was fraught with danger, as creatures emerged, their eyes gleaming with malice.

'Stay close,' Blair urged, her voice steady despite looming threats.

Kai nodded, his grip tightening on his sword.

Suddenly, a swarm of shadowy figures emerged from the darkness, their forms closing in on them. With a swift motion, Kai drew his sword, its blade shimmering. Blair summoned a vortex of flames to engulf their foes.

The battle was fierce, the clash of steel and the crackle of magic filled the air as Blair and Kai fought the darkness.

'We can't let them beat us,' Blair declared, her voice cutting through the chaos.

With strikes and powerful spells, they pushed back the shadows, their determination unyielding despite the relentless assault.

As the last of the figures fell, the two pressed on, their determination strong despite the challenges that lay ahead. Their journey led them deep into the heart of Ashen Plains, where the air seemed to pulse with dark energy, the ground trembling beneath them.

Finally, they reached the Shadow Phoenix's lair, a towering citadel of shadow that loomed ominously against the darkened sky.

'Ready yourself,' Blair said, her voice tinged with determination.

Kai nodded, his gaze steely, 'We've come this far. Let's finish this.'

With resolve burning in their hearts, Blair and Kai faced the final guardian before the Shadow Phoenix - a massive golem forged from the stones of the earth and imbued with darkness. As they prepared for their ultimate battle, their spirits burned bright with hope; they could bring an end to the Phoenix's reign of terror and restore peace.

In a blinding flash and the Shadow Phoenix's power in their grasp, Blair and Kai confronted him in a fierce battle. Despite the creature's overwhelming power, they fought with courage, refusing to surrender in despair. With a surge of hope, they unleashed the Phoenix's Feather powers, banishing the Shadow Phoenix into depths of darkness.

As the last echoes of the battle faded, the skies cleared, and the land was bathed in the warm glow of dawn. The once desolate Ashen Plains blossomed with a new life, and the people of Eldoria emerged, their hearts filled with hope.

Peace

By Diya Bachada - age 11

The thick, turbulent, smoky clouds loomed, spiralling above - ready to guzzle its prey, as the night unfurled its velvet cloak. There sat little Faith, under the towering oak tree, branches twisted and gnarled around her like grasping fingers. Dense trees flourished on all sides, shooting up high into the inky, starry night. A quilt of vines and lush leaves surged through the forest floor. Outgrown roots clawed through the forest, demolishing everything that lay in its path. After what seemed like a lifetime, the gunshots and explosions had finally stopped, though the pain would stay for evermore. She had lost everything. Her home had been bombed, her family had been killed, she was on her own now. The dead atmosphere made Faith shiver. She was wearing a scrawny, shabby dress, covered with moth-eaten holes and, where the patchwork had been mended, it was falling apart. Faith's feet were aching and throbbing with pain. She clutched her grubby rag doll and lifted the quilt over her.

A perfectly divine, glowing shooting star swept gracefully into the jet-black night sky. "All I wish for is peace," whispered Faith as she watched it elegantly travel into a pool of darkness.

Bang! Crash! Wallop!

The shimmer of light swerved around tree trunks, swiftly landing in the squelchy mud. Slowly, fatigued Faith hobbled towards the glow. An old plump wise man stood there, his eyes twinkling in the silver pale glow of the moonlight, engrossed in his surroundings. He was wrapped in sturdy armour, formed with a variety of cogs and coils, which had many patches where the armour had become tiresomely worn out. He had a fluffy, wispy, scruffy beard and a warm jolly smile.

"Is that your wish?" asked Faith .

"Once," replied the old man.

Gradually, he reached into his pocket and brought out a hand-carved flute, engraved with peculiar patterns. The flute was exceptionally soft and light and had an almost magical touch to it. Tranquilly, he picked up the flute and pressed it against his lips. A cheerful melody began to flow through the flute. The joyful tune surged through the town, spreading hope everywhere it travelled. Slowly, children emerged from the smouldering rubble of what was once their homes. Children poured onto the street gazing into the starry, inky night wishing, hoping for everything to go back to the way it was...wishing for peace. Suddenly, wishes gushed down from the sky. With each drop a burst of colour began to spread throughout the town.

Happiness filled the meek town once again.

Family Again

By Serena Humura -age 10

***Note**: The following story is true. Serena lived in Italy until eighteen months ago, when she was finally able to move to England to be with her father. The only English words she knew were, 'Hi', colours and numbers from one to ten. What an incredibly brave thing she did when she entered a creative writing competition in a language she'd only been learning for eighteen months! Many congratulations, Serena. You story is inspiring and a true testimony to the meaning of hope.* CB

Family Again

"Will my family ever be reunited?" Serena kept repeating the question every day to herself. Serena missed her dad very much. She dreamed that she could go to London with him. One day her mum saw that she was sad.

"What happened?" she asked.

"I miss Dad," Serena said.

Mum had a think. Suddenly, she had an idea. "Why don't you call your dad?" she said.

"Great idea!" Serena replied with a smile. Serena hugged her mum tightly.

From then on, every Saturday and Sunday, Serena called her dad. One Saturday, Serena's dad said to her, "One day, you will come to London with me."

She was so excited!

Then, that day came true. Serena went to London and saw her dad waiting for her. She ran up and hugged him. She was so happy, she cried.

After that, Serena and her family moved to London to be with their dad.

Once settled, Serena's dad said, "It's time to go to school."

Serena was so nervous, she did not even speak English! Serena told her dad that she was scared, but she was brave and went to school anyway. At school, Serena made her first friend, Fiona. Fiona helped her with her lessons and her English. Then Serena met some new friends – Maisie, Aliki, Reign, Aysen and Lilly. They are now her good friends, and they help her with everything!

Her best friend ever is Pary. Serena now is happy – she loves Cherry Tree School, and the hope it has given her. She also has her neighbours – Joy, Jed, Josh and Jessica. They help Serena's family too by sharing food and holding sleepovers.

Serena loves London, because now her life is there.

Stamina

By Lily Warren - age 10

My name is Elanor and this is my story.

It all started with my classmate Maya. She was such a snob, always bragging about herself in things that weren't even that cool. One of the things was how she won the hundred metre sprint. She was always showing off her glossy brown hair, and how it complemented the colour of gold in her medal.

Then a sheet appeared in the classroom, it was a cross country signup sheet. It was competitive, and the top three runners would make the new cross country school team. Only five children from each class would be picked. It was like a lottery. I was about to put my name up, when Maya and her gang shoved me out of the way. Maya wrote down her name and attached a heart to the end of it. She turned to me and sharply stared into my eyes.

"You're not actually signing your name up are you?" she laughed, flicking her hair in my eyes and strutting out with a parade of laughter behind her.

I glanced in a mirror at the back of the classroom. I looked the same, except I was standing on a podium with a medal around my neck. I looked ecstatic.

I looked away and I suddenly felt an urge *to beat Maya.*

I quickly ran towards the signup sheet and put my name down in my very best handwriting.

The next day, I rushed to the whiteboard and saw the students who had been selected for the cross country run. The list had five names on: Maya, Annabelle, a couple more and finally, at the bottom... me!

I was so excited!

I couldn't wait, and all day my heart was beating twice as fast as normal.

Then, there I was at the starting line in my green PE kit. The starter horn beeped and I set off. I ran. I ran as fast as I could, but then I collapsed before I was even half way round the course. I was so tired I was panting. A tall stranger from another school ran over to me.

"Use your breath wisely," she told me. "Try counting one, two, three, four and sync your legs to it. Breathe through your nose and out through your mouth. Use your stamina wisely, it helps."

She ran off. I looked down for a split second to catch my breath and when I looked up, she had disappeared.

I got up and started running again, listening to her voice telling me how to breathe better. The next thing I knew, I was at the finish line. The tall stranger was there, smiling at me as we got our competitor medals.

I didn't need to worry about Maya and her friends anymore, as I had found an amazing best friend in Sophia, the stranger from the race.

And to think that it was all just me hoping to get selected in the first place...

Amber, Where Did You Go?

By Ruby England - age 11

A long time ago, I entered the place that felt everlong, the orphanage. My greatest wish was to have a loving family. I was eight-years-old and all I hoped for was a family.

One day, I was on grocery duty with my best friend Amber and Mrs Forte, the *really* annoying, strict teacher who no one liked. We headed back through the black, metal gates and walked up to the dull maroon brick wall. Our hands tightly held the plastic bags full of food while Mrs Forte opened the large, heavy door with her black staff key card. Amber and I dragged our feet to the cafeteria and dropped our bags on the floor. As quick as a flash, we dashed across the halls, running towards the girls' room. Once we entered, we started to jot down ideas on how to escape.

"Maybe we should just leave it, Amber, it's really not worth it." I whispered, making sure the security cameras didn't hear me. Amber begged and begged and begged so much that it got on my nerves, and normally nothing really makes me mad.

We were called down for dinner, but no one went. I felt bad for everyone, even those who I shouldn't feel bad for. I explained to the girls about how the staff spent time making the food, so we should go. Lola and Mia agreed to come with me, but no one else did.

We finished up after about a quarter of an hour eating soggy food and went straight up to the girls' room. Mia opened the doors widely while Lola and I each carried four pieces of bread in our arms for the others.

No-one was there.

Mia sprinted to check the bathrooms while Lola and I searched the room. I peered through the window and saw Jess, Maria, Zoe, Poppy, Jasmine, Kayla and Emma, running away from the orphanage, but no Amber. I screeched, "Wherever you are, Amber, don't leave me here. Amber please, I beg you!"

When I was eleven, I thought I'd never recover. I couldn't even remember Amber's face anymore, but I always hoped to find her.

Then I found her. I found Amber. My new parents posted everywhere on social media to help me find her and one day she was found. She even remembered me.

I couldn't believe my dream came true.

The Tale of the Inseparable

By Izzy Rawle - age 9

Once, there were two best friends. A ginger cat named Zoe and a scruffy sheep dog named Dani.

But they had a problem.

They were both homeless. Both lived in an alleyway in Cardiff, Wales. Both wanted a home.

One day, Dani waited in front of the alleyway, and someone took him away. But Dani didn't want to go without Zoe. He wanted to go back for her.

For the next few days, Dani missed Zoe. Although Dani had a nice new home, he wasn't happy without Zoe.

One day, when Dani was on a walk, he saw the alleyway and persuaded his owner to go in. So they did, but Zoe wasn't there and sadly, Dani went back home.

The next day, Dani and his owner were invited to visit their neighbour's new cat.

"It won't be nearly as kind as Zoe," thought Dani. But he was wrong. It was Zoe! Zoe and Dani were so excited to be neighbours.

"I knew we would both find a home one day," said Zoe.

"And you were right," said Dani.

So, for the rest of their lives, Dani and Zoe lived in a home where someone actually cared for them.

There is always hope.

A Lion Called Carter

By Shaan Voralia - age 10

Once upon a time, there lived an enthusiastic lion called Carter. Carter had lost his family in an attack by armed hunters. As the sun faded away, the lonely lion soullessly walked into the distance with a huge frown on his face.

The one thing that Carter prayed for was zebra pie, because it was extremely moist and flavorsome. His razor-sharp teeth could destroy his prey in seconds! All he needed were the ingredients for his delicious, succulent meal: salt, bread, raw rabbit, blood and most importantly...raw zebra.

Whilst Carter marched deeper into the blazing hot savanna, he came face to face with a zebra who looked like it had plenty of energy and was dancing in the most peculiar way. Without thinking, the lion pounced at the zebra whilst snarling horrifyingly. Skidding across the sand, the lion groaned in agony from the pain in the joints of his legs while the zebra sprinted across the piping hot savanna and through a river. Carter, unfortunately, was afraid of water. As the zebra galloped away, the lion roared outrageously in disappointment.

All of a sudden, a whittering entered Carter's ears. It got louder, and louder and LOUDER until three shadows appeared.

"Who's the...the...there?" stuttered the lion. Out popped a meerkat, followed by a monkey, followed by a snake. Carter stood very still. He wondered, could these fellows be friends or foes? How did they get here?

Suddenly, all three of them said, "Hello! Who are you? You look hungry. We can get you the juiciest fruits in the whole of the savanna, if you want?"

"Yes please!" growled Carter, softly.

"Then come with us," said the meerkat.

As they wandered towards the fruit tree, Carter got to the know the trio and, for the first time in ages, he laughed. After Carter filled his face with delicious fruits, his new friends took him to their home.

After a couple of weeks, Carter thought to himself, "This is a fresh start! My hopes and dreams of having food, having friends and no longer being lonely came true! Everything I hoped for has come true!"

"Thank the Lord for saving me from starving to death!" whispered Carter, with a smile on his face.

As the little shadows appeared behind Carter, he turned and began to thank the wonderful creatures for saving him and for looking after him. Suddenly all four animals heard a growl behind them. Unexpectedly, a hyena jumped out of the bushes and started to circle the four creatures as a cheeky grin slithered across his face.

"We're going to die!" cried the monkey.

"Don't be babies, we are not going to die," hissed the brave snake.

"Bet that?" smirked the hyena with sarcasm.

All of a sudden, the snake attacked the hyena and left a nasty bruise.

"That's what you get, you filthy animal!" laughed the snake.

Luckily for them, no one dared to mess with them again!

The Bear Cub of Bluebell Wood

By Aoife Coggins - age 8

One snowy day, two girls were strolling in Bluebell Wood, chatting happily as they crunched through the icy snow. Suddenly, Jasmine saw something out of the corner of her eye and she turned and gasped, "Daisy, Daisy, look I see something. It's a cave, come on!" Daisy hurried after her.

The cave was glowing with sparkles and they saw a glimpse of something behind a rock. What was it? Who was it? Where was the rest of its family? What was it doing in the cave? The questions swirled round in the girls' heads.

"Look!" whispered Jasmine in a frightened tone.

"It looks like a bear cub!" exclaimed Daisy in a super excited tone. "Oh the poor thing, looks like it hasn't eaten for weeks," cried the girls. It had soft matted fur, big caramel, chocolatey eyes and a shiny wet nose. It stood there, whimpering in the cold.

Daisy smashed a hole in the ice of the nearby frozen river, picked up two frozen fish and put them just above where they had seen the bear cub. The cub's little round eyes peeped over the rock, staring at the fish longingly. The children nodded and Jasmine said in her softest voice, "Go on, eat it, it's yours". Suddenly, she noticed a small heart shaped pebble the little cub was clasping tightly. Daisy saw it too.

"Why do you think he carries that?" asked Jasmine. "He may carry it for hope of finding his long lost family if they're still out there." She spoke in a low tone for fear the little bear would hear her words and get upset.

Jasmine glanced at her watch. "Oh no! It's 9.30, Daisy, we have to go!" The little bear burst into tears. The girls felt sorry for the small bear and promised to come back tomorrow with more fish and to help the little guy find his family.

So, the next day, the girls ran back, ploughing through the icy snow, dragging an enormous barrel of fish on their sledge. When they got to the cave, the little bear ate hungrily, longing, hoping, dreaming that he would soon be reunited with his family. The girls decided to search for the bear's family and set off on a long journey through forests, jumping over stepping stones across running rivers. Both girls were determined to reunite the little bear with his family. Most of the time, the little bear had to be carried, for he could not run as fast as the girls, but when he could, he'd be bounding behind them.

Finally, they came to a large tree. As soon as the bear touched the tree trunk, flowers burst from every bud and a hole appeared. They crawled through, and on the other side, the bear's family was waiting for his return. It was time to say goodbye and set off on the long journey home.

Remember, when all seems to be lost, there is always hope!

The Race Within

By Bianca Vasvari - age 12

His skin was beginning to ache. The trees dipped down their branches and the greenness of the trees, which seemed to be a wall of colour up close, didn't seem green at all. His mind sank with the weight of the pressures of the worries and expectations.

"On your marks. Get set. GO!"

Silence.

In his mind, the voices seemed to disappear, the track luminescing in his eyes, blocked by the shadows of the people in front of him as the runners took off. Feet ahead of him went further away into the distance, opening a glowing entrance of the track. What had once been a huddle of keen runners was now a scattered flock of birds, ready to fly. His legs stung with pain as his chest started to compress. Eyes vivid with tears and the world spinning around him. *Don't give up, you're so close.* The memories of those words kept coming, slowly, repeatedly returning to his mind. How could he possibly catch up with the people ahead?

Through the blurry eyes, a vivid image of black and white came creeping closer. Relief swept over him, tears streaming down from his eyes. Years of trial and practice, and he was still just there inhaling their wins and trophies. But it was over.

Back at home, surrounded by endless dry grass, endlessly breathing arid air, just like a Sahara desert of dreams. The warm smell of bread rolls and fresh soup wafted in his nose, and the touch of water on his taste buds felt like an angel lying on his tongue. He went to sleep.

Beep! Beep! The alarm clock rang furiously, time to get up? Eight o'clock!

He was sure he had set it for six. He was so late! Rushing to get dressed, he ran towards the local field and met up with his coach. He wanted to get better. He trained for hours on end, focusing on one goal. To win.

'He breaks another record again. Can anyone beat this man?'

'He is so good that he is the icon of the year. Cheers to that!'

'Will he ever retire? Do we want him to?'

'The BBC have a number of questions to ask you: Do you see yourself continuing this sport?'

A few years later, he entered a marathon. Everyone cheered his name. Ambitious journalists ready to record another spectacular triumph, were rapidly writing up their perspectives of the race.

"On your marks. Get set. GO!"

Readier than ever, he flew past the runners, creating fire under his feet. The pain swelled up, but that was no match for the energy left inside of him. His arms competed against the wind. The tape snapped as he crossed the finish line. His shorts and top were slithery with sweat. A broken record, once again. This was who he was, showing everyone that you can come from anywhere, yet here he was, fulfilling dreams.

This was Usain Bolt...

Hope

By Pavaki Singh - age 10

Immigration has been the hardest thing I have ever experienced in my life. Losing my mum and having a sick sister wasn't easy at all. It all started when our city was being bombed. My sister Sara, my mother, my father and I became fugitives as we escaped from our country. Primarily, we took a boat filled with over a hundred people, but this was where our mother died. Shockingly, Mother was knocked off when more people boarded the boat and she drowned. An agony gripped our hearts and spread through our bodies until we felt like we were going to explode. After this haunting tragedy of our lives, we decided to not travel by boat anymore, but that was calamitous, because we spent weeks walking; we didn't even know where to go. We could only do one thing: hope.

Walking wasn't too bad until Sara caught a lung infection; she could barely breathe. Luckily, not long after, we stumbled upon a lorry that would take us to our new homeland. It only took us a couple of days to get to the place we would live. As soon as we arrived, we rushed to the hospital since Sara's breathing was getting worse.

The doctors announced, "We have diagnosed her with pneumonia. Generally we would be able to treat it, but since she has had it for a while and hasn't come straight to hospital, her chances are slim."

A kaleidoscope of emotions enveloped me: hope that my sister would get better, trepidation that another member of my family might pass and sorrow for what my sister was going through. Knowing that my little sister could pass was the worst thing ever. Fear settled on me like a dark fog, bringing a chill that crept over me that no amount of heat could drive away!

Father and I were determined that Sara would get better, but there wasn't a high chance that she would. Astonishingly, the doctor told us that we were allowed to take her out for a day, because she was getting better. The one thing we have wanted to do since we came here was go to the beach, and now was the time we could. We went there and had the best time in the world. We all had our first ice-cream and made our first sandcastle. The day had passed and we went back to the hospital. Outstandingly, the doctor had cleared Sara from the hospital and told us that she was free to do whatever she wanted as long as she was precautious of her health. That was when Father and I realised that hope is real and does come true...

The moral of this story is, 'The one thing in life you should never lose is hope.' 'Umeed par duniya kayam hai,' is a famous Hindi proverb, which means, 'The world is built of hope'.

Hope is one of the most pivotal things in life...

About the Editor

Caroline likes making things.

Here are some of the things she likes to make: children, homes for lost dogs, exciting books, parties, trips to the seaside/theatre/school (yes, really!) and chocolate cake, although she prefers to eat it.

More books by Caroline...

The Runaway Children of Chennai

The Secret Children of Mumbai

The Secret Life of Dmitri Molchalin

The Mole of Moscow, June 2024

The Fox of Sevastopol, November 2024

Crazy Creatives – how to write a brilliant short story, October 2024

Subscribe to Caroline's blog so you don't miss the next book

www.carolineboxall.com

Short Story Competition 2025

Enter Caroline's short story competition to win a place in a real, published book!

Rules

- Open to children aged 8-13
- Write a short story with a theme of ***Courage*** in up to 500 words (see tips @ CarolineBoxall.com)
- Edit and improve
- Send your story to CarolineBoxall@hotmail.co.uk by 1st May (go to CarolineBoxall.com for more details)
- Sign up to the website here where the winners will be announced on 1st June

GOOD LUCK!

Printed in Great Britain
by Amazon

46123942R00067